Foreword by Air Officer Commanding-In-Chief Personnel and Training Command Air Chief Marshal Sir David Cousins KCB AFC BA RAF

'A Trip down Memory Lane'

Recent years have witnessed the closure of a number of well known Royal Air Force stations. Each closure is understandably clouded with sadness for all who are serving there at the time and for those who have been associated with the unit in the past. It is so important, therefore, that in closing RAF Locking every effort is made to keep alive those moments in history there that people will remember with pride and enjoyment.

This book has been extensively researched. The author has visited museums and the Air Historical Branch, read Boy Entrant and Apprentice Association's histories, and interviewed countless men and women who served on the Station. The result is an excellent read and a warm and welcome trip down memory lane for those who have worked among the huts and 'T Blocks'.

Finally, I am particularly pleased to support this project as all proceeds will go to the Royal Air Force Association, an organisation which serves so well all those airmen and officers who are in need of support. I commend the book highly to you.

Thanks

Many, many thousands of people have spent their formative years within the Royal Air Force Locking training machine. There is no doubt that the people who were trained here have contributed much to the Royal Air Force and their sense of service and commitment was, in no small part, generated by the 'conditioning' received while under training. With the Station closing it was considered that the history of this place and the people who served here ought to be put on record for posterity before it was lost forever and should reflect the ethos and culture and not be a cold facts and figures exercise.

The intention, therefore, was to tell the history of Royal Air Force Locking through the eyes of the people who served or were trained here, using the memories of 'old boys' and archive material written at the time. Using that basis for information there will undoubtedly be gaps where some important events have not been reported simply because no one has written the story down, or it has been written and lost, and the official history has not deemed it worthy of inclusion. Also, memories being what they are, it is likely that someone somewhere reading this book will spot an occasional error of fact. To illustrate this, many people told me the story of the tragic accident involving the double decker bus on the Locking Moor Road, however, the date has ranged from 1946, the actual date, to 1963, with the aircraft type changing to suit the date. So please forgive any unintentional errors and accept the record of the story even if the mists of time have shrouded some of the detail.

My thanks and appreciation are extended to all the contributors who have taken a lot of trouble to write down their memories, not an easy task as stories are much easier to tell than write, and for the loan of their extremely valuable archive photographs and other material. This book could not have been written without your support and I take great pleasure in mentioning people by name in the text, where appropriate, and also by recording the names of everyone who contributed at the back of the book.

Furthermore, writing this book has been a team effort. So it is with pleasure that I record my appreciation to the following people who have made a significant contribution to the production of this book and without whose efforts this project would not have been completed: Gp Capt Simon Rooms for the original concept, his unwavering support, endless proof reading and for allowing me the time to complete this work. Flt Lt Chris Stevens for the marketing and sales of the book. Chf Tech Greg Burns for his support in office, research and for liaising with the publishers. Mr Graham Day (Air Historical Branch) for researching information and for helping me find my way through the archives. Mr Tony Marriot (Command Graphics) for his excellent cartoons. Mrs Kate Morgan for local research in newspaper and museum archives, and finally, to my wife, Mrs Bonnie Tillbrook for spending days proof reading and editing, for accepting that her dining room has been encumbered with unsorted material and for managing to continue to live with me and 'the book'.

Sqn Ldr Ray Tillbrook

Thanks are also due to the book's official sponsors: The Royal Air Forces Association and Rolls-Royce

Dedication

This book is dedicated to all those Service personnel, civilians and their families who have served Royal Air Force Locking during the Station's long and illustrious history. Their efforts as members of the permanent staff, as trainees and students or as members of the general public have together made a major contribution to this country's well-being by providing the Royal Air Force, and the Fleet Air Arm, with high calibre mechanics and technicians who have proved themselves worthy of the uniform on innumerable occasions.

Royal Air Force Locking Station Commanders

Gp Capt NC Spratt	1939-40
Gp Capt F Fernihough	1940-41
Gp Capt JM Glaisher	1941-43
Gp Capt AE Paish	1943-44
Gp Capt JD St Leger	1944-46
Gp Capt AE Paish	1946-49
Gp Capt RB Harrison	1949-50
Gp Capt HA Evans-Evans	1950-52
Gp Capt AT Monks	1952-53
Gp Capt B Robinson	1953-55
Gp Capt DN Kington-Blair-Oliphant	1955-58
Gp Capt AP Chamberlain	1958-59
Air Cdre HG Leonard-Williams	1959-61
Air Cdre W D Disbrey	1961-64
Air Cdre CRC Howlett	1964-65
Gp Capt AF Ward	1965-66
Air Cdre C S Betts	1966-67
Gp Capt NW Maskell	1967-69
Gp Capt FC Padfield	1969-71
Gp Capt W Ormrod	1971-74
Gp Capt FM Holroyd	1974-76
Gp Capt JM Walker	1976-77
Gp Capt PJ Hector	1977-80
Gp Capt DG Harrington	1980-82
Gp Capt KG Lewis	1982-84
Gp Capt MRM Heyes	1984-87
Gp Capt RCR Johnston	1987-89
Gp Capt RJ Holt	1989-91
Gp Capt CM Davison	1991-93
Gp Capt I Sloss	1993-95
Gp Capt WS Rooms	1995-present

Contents

A Brief History of RAF Locking from 1939	2
The War and Immediate Post War Years	5
Tales from the 'Old Boys'	8
The Local Community	22
Boy Entrants	24
The Parable of the Erkites	41
RAF Locking's own Roman Villa	42
Training Times	45
Events of the Time	56
Fireside WAAFS	58
Cadet Camps	59
Ceremonial	61
The Station Mascot	64
The Training of Aircraft Apprentices	65
The Locking Apprentice	71
Rescues	88
The Western Band of the RAF	90
RAF Amateur Radio Society	97
Connections with the Royal Family	98
Aircraft at RAF Locking	102
The Great Rebuilding Plan	105
Let the Doors Be Opened	109
Modern Training	110
Thoughts from a Direct Entry Fitter	115
A Day in the Life of an Airman	118
Operation Burberry 1977/78	120
The Weston Flood Disaster	120
Flowerdown Fair	122
The B.S.A.D. Wheelchair Marathon	128
Noteworthy Events of the Time	129
Our Airmen	133
Acknowledgements	134

Editorial Director: Ron Pearson
Sub-editor: Joanne Grove
Advertising Sales: Ursula Taylor

© This magazine contains official information and should be treated with discretion by the recipient. No responsibility for the quality of goods or services advertised in this magazine can be accepted by the publishers or printers. Advertisements are included in good faith. Published by Forces and Corporate Publishing Ltd, Hamblin House, Hamblin Court, 92-94 High Street, Rushden, Northamptonshire NN10 OPQ. Tel: 01933 419994. Fax: 01933 419584.

Over and Out 1

A Brief History of RAF Locking

Royal Air Force Locking has always been a training school since it opened in 1939, but the type of training offered and the ages and specialisations of trainees has changed several times. While the Station has remained open continuously, the scale of activities was considerably reduced in the late 1940s, until the arrival of No. 1 Radio School. Indeed, it is with this school that life at RAF Locking is always associated.

On 2 January 1939 a party of seven officers formally opened No 5 School of Technical Training. By April, the Station's strength had grown to over 1,700 servicemen and 11 civilian education officers. Within the three Training Wings, No 5 SofTT trained servicemen of the RAF and Fleet Air Arm in the niceties of parachute packing, fabric working and provided trade training to Flight Mechanics and Riggers.

By March 1943 there were four workshops covering an area of 50,400 square feet (still in existence today) and four Bellman Hangers covering 6,648 square feet. Within that three years 30,682 airmen had been trained. The scale of the operation was enormous and RAF Locking was a huge hutted encampment supporting many thousands of airmen and sailors under training. It was not unusual to have 6,000 personnel on parade at any one time.

Reduced

After the war the scale of the training was progressively reduced until eventually No 5 SofTT closed on 15 May 1950. Ten days later RAF Locking was transferred to No 27 Group, Training Command to become the home of No. 1 Radio School. The full history of No 1 RS has been published as part of its 50th Anniversary celebrations in 1993, sufficient to say here that No 1 RS had been in existence since 1943 at RAF Cranwell having developed from a School for Wireless Operators formed at Farnborough in 1915.

To show a complete picture, it is necessary to explain briefly the various schemes of training which, over time, have had a direct influence on how life was conducted at RAF Locking (each area is covered in more detail in later chapters). Moreover, to confuse the picture, some of the schemes overlapped the change of ownership in 1950 and the move from RAF Cranwell.

In 1946 the Government of the day decided to re-introduce the pre-war Boy Entrant training scheme. Demobilisation at the end of the war was creating resettlement and training problems for many employers who were not able to offer training for school leavers, so the introduction of the Boy Entrant scheme was seen as a social provision at the time.

Significant

As it happens, the scheme had a significant impact on the Royal Air Force because of the quality of recruit, who provided the backbone of the trained manpower for many years to come. The scheme provided basic recruit training and technical training in the many facets of aircraft engineering, both academic and practical. No 1 Entry, of 370 recruits, arrived at RAF Locking in May of 1947 and graduated in November 1948. The First to Fifth Entries completed all their training at RAF Locking, while the Sixth to Tenth Entries either completed their training, or were wholly trained, at RAF Cosford, after which the scheme was discontinued.

RAF Apprentice Training was started in 1922 and during the war was concentrated at RAF Cranwell. After the war No 1 RS, then at RAF Cranwell, provided training in the radio and radar trades for apprentices, National Servicemen and regular airmen.

In October 1950 the majority of the school

> 'As it happens, the (Boy Entrant) scheme had a significant impact on the Royal Air Force because of the quality of recruit, who provided the backbone of the trained manpower for many years to come.'

moved to RAF Locking while the remainder at RAF Cranwell, concerned only with apprentice training, was renamed No 6 Radio School. However, on 1 December 1950 the RAF Cranwell element disbanded and its apprentices rejoined No 1 RS at RAF Locking. The first aircraft apprentices to graduate were No 64 Entry on 18 December 1952. In the early 1950s apprenticeships were undertaken at both RAF Locking and at RAF Halton and were of three years duration. At RAF Locking there were three intakes of about 100 strong each year. The three year aircraft apprentice training ended in 1966, to be replaced by shorter craft (one year) and technician (two year) apprenticeships. Apprentice training at RAF Locking finally ceased in March 1976 with the passing out of the 122nd Entry.

Complexity

The 1964 trade structure was introduced to meet the growing complexity of aircraft and electronic systems. In particular, the impending arrival of TSR2 showed that the reliance on maintenance by repair had to end. It was superseded by the concept of repair by replacement and all engineering trades were affected by this change in policy. As a result, the single skilled Aircraft Apprentice was replaced with the Technician Apprentice whose three year training covered the whole spectrum of the trade. Graduating to the rank of Corporal, he passed out with an ONC which gave him a considerable advantage over the former Locking Apprentices.

Also as part of the 1964 trade structure review, Craft Apprentices were introduced to ~~need~~ for skilled craftsmen. These schemes were introduced for the previous single skill trades with a reduced course length of two years. Finally, driven again by the needs of aircraft engineering rather than the needs of the communications electronics trade group, Mechanic Apprentices were introduced. Their training, with a course length of one year, commenced in 1970 but only lasted for five entries.

In 1965, aircraft direct entry and apprentice training moved to the No 2 School of Technical Training at RAF Cosford leaving the ground electronics specialisations at RAF Locking within the No 1 Radio School.

For the record:
- The final Aircraft Apprentice Entry was the 106th, which passed out in 1966.
- The first Technician Apprentice Entry was the 107th passing out in 1967 and the final Entry was the 122nd who passed out in 1976.
- The first Mechanic Apprentice Entry was the 402nd and the final Entry was the 406th which passed out in 1972.
- The first two Craft Apprentice Entries, the 201st and 202nd, graduated in 1966 and the final Entry, the 231st, completed their training in 1974.

The Direct Entry Fitter scheme was introduced in 1972 for the multi skilled Ground Communications and Ground Radar trades, the Synthetic Trainer trade being added to the scheme in 1976.

A further reorganisation occurred in 1976

> 'The 1964 Trade Structure was introduced to meet the growing complexity of aircraft and electronic systems. In particular, the impending arrival of TSR2 showed that the reliance on maintenance by repair had to end. It was superseded by the concept of repair by replacement and all engineering trades were affected by this change in policy.'

Over and Out 3

A Brief History of RAF Locking from 1939

when the Ground Electronics Trade was split further into Airfields, Radar and Communications sub trades. This introduced the one year single skill Direct Entry Fitter who graduated as junior technicians and a shorter course for mechanics who graduated as senior aircraftmen, but who could by selection return later to complete their fitters course.

The end of the Cold War has resulted in significant reductions in RAF manpower and the closure of many stations. This has had a major impact on the training task; in 1990 there were about 1,000 trainees whereas now there are less than 400. Moreover, the future remains uncertain as civilianisation and contractorisation of jobs continues to threaten the size of TG3.

The technology and the nature of the operational task also continued to change, with equipment becoming more reliable, more sophisticated yet less easy to repair using traditional techniques. The RAF concluded that it was over training its tradesmen on entry to the service and that many tasks could be carried out by a mechanic. Accordingly in 1993 the trade group was again rationalised to form a single ground electronics trade with all new recruits entering as mechanics with an opportunity for further training to obtain a fitter qualification.

Reduced

As the size of the RAF has reduced, the need for electronic specialists has increased and this has resulted in a shift in the balance between basic training and specialist equipment, Pre-Employment Training (PET). Here, officers and airmen are trained on a wide variety of courses ranging in length from a few days to six months or more covering virtually all the RAF's ground electronics equipment and systems, as well as computing and software engineering. Nowadays, this latter training forms the backbone of the school and mature students are in the majority. Also Trade Management Training, an intense blend of theory and practice, gives the newly promoted Corporal and Sergeant the management skills they will need as supervisors and junior line managers.

Although the emphasis at RAF Locking has always been on the training of engineering technicians and mechanics, that is no longer completely true today. In 1989 the training of the Trade Group 11 - Communications Operating Trades moved to RAF Locking from their home at RAF Cosford. This trade is a direct descendant of the Wireless Operators whose training can be traced back through various training schools to 1915.

'The end of the Cold War has resulted in significant reductions in RAF manpower and the closure of many stations. This has had a major impact on the training task; in 1990 there were about 1,000 trainees whereas now there are less than 400.'

At the end of World War Two, operator training had been concentrated at RAF Compton Basset and expanded to include teleprinter operator, telephonist and telegraphist. On the closure of RAF Compton Basset training moved to RAF Cosford and in 1981 the training was modernised to become Telecommunications Operator - TCO trade. In a sense the wheel has now come a full circle with operator training back at the RAF's last Radio School.

Changes

Through time, training at RAF Locking has re-invented itself many times to reflect the enormous technical and cultural changes that have occurred in the last 60 years. The training offered at RAF Locking has always been second to none and this is evident in the number of graduates who have reached high office both inside and outside the Royal Air Force, in turn making a significant contribution to the well-being of the nation, reflecting the truth of the RAF Locking motto:

Docemus - We Teach.

The War and Immediate Post War Years

Written by Wg Cdr Peter Squires in 1988

Early beginnings

On 2 January 1939 a small party of seven officers formally opened 5 SofTT RAF Locking, under the temporary command of Wg Cdr Glaisher DFC. Within five days over 200 airmen arrived from Henlow and before they had time to draw breath they were formally inspected by the CinC 24 Group on 24 January. From March until April the Station's strength grew to over 1,700 Servicemen and 11 civilian education officers. Over 1,000 airmen came from Henlow, and 293 naval ratings from RAF St Athan and Manston. The Station formed itself into three wings: No 1 Wing trained fabric workers and parachute packers and Nos 2 and 3 Wing trained flight mechanics and flight riggers.

Chaotic

The arrival of so many men must have been chaotic. Imagine the scene which led to this statement in the Station's Operations Record Book (ORB) on 3 March 1939, 'Two special trains arrived at Milton Halt from Henlow.

Richie Richardson in this photograph arrived at Milton Halt in September 1939

The declaration of war

Airmen and naval ratings were marched from the railway station to Locking. There was no parade ground and the workshops were incomplete.'

By June 1939 each Wing was training some 900 men, approximately half of whom were RN ratings. On 3 September 1939 the ORB reads, 'Declaration of war by Great Britain on Germany at 1100 hrs.' All ranks were informed they were on active service, issued with anti-gas clothing and air-raid precautions increased. The working week was divided into 11 half-days with the 'extra' half day spent on War Training. Christmas leave of six days was taken in 1939 - this was to be reduced to only one day in later years.

In January 1940 Leading Trainee appointments were announced by the Station Commander; they wore two horizontal stripes on their uniform and their role was to assist NCO's with the maintenance of discipline. By June 1940 the hospital had 150 beds and in the same month the Station held its first District Court Martial - two airmen were charged with running a lottery, one was awarded 156 days detention and the charge against the second was dismissed. How things have changed - nowadays such prize draws are a prime source of fund-raising.

Air-raid warnings intensified in June and July 1940 and the Station prepared to defend itself against sabotage and external attack. On 14 August 1940 the

> *'Air-raid warnings intensified in June and July 1940 and the Station prepared to defend itself against sabotage and external attack. On 14 August the Station was attacked by enemy aircraft.'*

Over and Out 5

The War and Immediate Post War Years

Station was attacked by enemy aircraft. The ORB reports, 'Two whistling bombs fell short one mile north-east of the Station. No damage was done to RAF personnel or property.' September 1940 saw considerable bombing around the camp. Locking was not hit, but damage was recorded at Worle, Banwell and the railway bridge near Weston Airport. Two houses in Weston and the telephone exchange at Banwell were wrecked.

On 8 September there was an invasion scare and the ringing of bells in Bristol was heard at Locking. The body of an enemy airman was washed up at Weston and the Station's machine gun defences were tested. October saw intense enemy aircraft activity with some 14 bombs landing near the camp including incendiaries on Hutton Hill. Two RAF aircraft crashed nearby after engaging the enemy and on 24 November 1940 Bristol suffered a very big air attack.

Although the number of air raids decreased in December 1940 the intensity of the individual raids increased and Bristol and South Wales were heavily bombed. The attacks did not abate and in January 1941 Weston was particularly hard-hit and Locking's airmen helped the local fire-fighting and rescue authorities. In February 1941 over 1,000 recruits arrived in Weston and in April, No 5 Recruiting Training Wing was formed in the Beach Hotel, Weston-super-Mare. On 9 August 1941 an Anti-Gas Parade was held. Gas masks (respirators to younger readers) were worn for 30 minutes while the Station Commander lectured the Parade on anti-gas measures (I wonder if the airmen heard him!). The Parade marched off wearing respirators.

Back-tracking in time, by the end of 1940 the Station's strength was 4,728 including 109 civilian instructors. The first WAAFs arrived in August 1940 for code and cypher duties and the WAAF Officers' Mess was opened in July 1941.

Importance

HRH Gp Capt Duke of Kent visited Locking in July 1940 and again in April 1941 when he was an air commodore. Marshal of the RAF, Lord Trenchard, founder of the Royal Air Force, also visited the Station twice - August 1941 and again in August 1942. The status of these visitors surely underlines the importance of Locking during the early part of the war.

In May 1941 No 4 Wing was formed to run conversion courses and perhaps to confuse the enemy the wings were renumbered 441, 442, 443 and 444 in September 1941.

At 0340 hrs on the 8 December 1941 hostilities were announced against Japan and in March 1942 Locking was ordered to arm its airmen with pikes! Perhaps this was a late counter to the local Army Commander who, in September 1940, regarded the 3,200 unarmed airmen in training at RAF Locking as 'useless bodies' who should be evacuated. It was in September 1940 that the civilian staff at Locking formed themselves into a local Home Guard Unit.

Enemy attacks were increasing again by April 1942 and on 27 and 28 June 1942 damage in Weston-super-Mare by enemy aircraft caused the cancellation of a parade to celebrate the third anniversary of the formation of the WAAF. In August 1942 enemy aircraft flew over Locking and 43 civilians were killed in raids on Bristol.

The training

The training of RN ratings ceased at the end of 1942. During the four years of No 5 Sof TT's existence from January 1939, 5,710 RN ratings passed through training.

By March 1943 the organisation seemed to have settled down sufficiently for the following statement to be made, 'No 5S of TT is devoted to the training of Flight Mechanics Airframe and Engines, Fitters Marine and Carpenters Boat Builder. Four workshops covering an area of 50,400 square feet. Four Bellman hangars each covering 6,648 square feet. Total output

---

'Enemy attacks were increasing again by April 1942 and on 27 and 28 June, damage in Weston-super-Mare by enemy aircraft caused the cancellation of a parade to celebrate the Third Anniversary of the formation of the WAAF. In August 1942 enemy aircraft flew over Locking and 43 civilians were killed in raids on Bristol.'

The War and Immediate Post War Years

since formation of unit 30,682.'

On 1 June 1943 Weston-super-Mare Airfield was transferred from No 10 Group Fighter Command to RAF Station Locking No 24 Group Technical Training Command and placed under the command of the Station Commander. Sections of Bristol Aircraft Factory and Weston Airways Factory were accommodated on the airfield.

In June 1943 the first WAAF Flight Mechanic course started and there were so many WAAF MT drivers that a 10 day course was introduced on the stripping and assembling of three types of internal combustion engines. There must have been plenty of WAAF's around even in 1941 because in September of that year Locking's WAAF Trumpet Band was formed.

Look no further than 10 September 1943 for beginnings of the L Tech ST trade for it is on this date that the Synthetic Control Trainer was introduced at Locking to 'replicate the landing of an actual machine.'

In September 1943 Saturday afternoon games was changed to PT spread throughout the week to reduce wear and tear on the Station's sports grounds.

Locking was also the home of No 1 RAF Works School formed on 1 January 1943 which ran a Field Engineering Course and a Field Flight Course. These were four week courses training personnel in both setting up Advanced Landing Grounds, and in demolition. By December 1943 this became No 1 School of Airfield Construction. The RAF Regiment was also at Locking in strength forming No 4 (Gunners) Wing in August 1942 which became RAF Regiment Wing in October 1942 running an Anti-Aircraft Practice Camp.

The large Station Hospital had 157 beds by March 1943 and the staff contributed a paper to the Lancet entitled 'March Fractures' - I wonder if Initial Officer Training staff know that their so-called lower-limb injuries problem was discovered at Locking 45 years ago!

The first intake of flight engineers started training in No 3 Wing in February 1944 and on 27 March 1944, during an enemy air raid, a canister of incendiaries was dropped on Weston Airfield just before midnight. One Oxford aircraft was slightly damaged by

Marching to Work

splinters.

In April and May 1944 well over 500 Americans arrived for firing practice on Brean Ranges. By the time No 1 Anti-Aircraft Practice Camp closed in August 1944 over three and a half million rounds of .303 and nearly three quarter million rounds of 20mm had been fired, 1944 also saw the arrival of Polish and Italian Servicemen at the School.

Locking's ties with the Royal Navy were renewed in March 1945 when Headquarters 24 Group tasked No 5 SofTT with converting two intakes of 500 airmen from Fitter II (E), Fitter II (A), Flight Mechanics (E) and Flight Mechanics (A) to the corresponding Fleet Air Arm trades.

In 1945 No 5S of TT was running the following courses: Aircraft Finishers (eight weeks), Cleaning and Handling Transparent Plastics (one week), Jet Propelled Engines (two weeks), Fitter II (E) (16 weeks), Fitter II (A) (14 weeks), Conversion Courses - Flight Mechanic (A) to Fitter II (A) RAF, Naval Conversion Courses (three weeks), Officers' Mess Stewardess (three weeks) and Advanced Cooks Course (eight weeks).

VE Day and beyond

For 8 and 9 May 1945, VE Day and VE+1 Day, Locking's ORB states, 'The Station Commander addressed the Station on VE Day and Sunday routine was observed for the rest of that day and VE+1 Day. Admission to the Station cinema was free on VE Day and a band concert and dance were held. Despite pessimistic forecasts no cases of indiscipline occurred. One NCO absented himself for two days at the end of his leave stating he misconstrued the broadcast announcement made by the BBC.'

Fascinating

Locking was then selected as one of the Stations at which the RAF was 'At Home' and on 15 September 1945, 2,000 civilians visited the camp. No refreshments were served, there was virtually no transport available from Weston-super-Mare (perhaps not surprising with food and petrol rationing) and the visitors were split into parties and conducted around the Camp by guides. Extracts from the local newspapers are quite fascinating. Initial reports are full of praise for the accommodation, the local cafe (the NAAFI), the Station cinema, the churches, the libraries, the ingenious training aids and 'those light-hearted lads who once walked our streets, mixed with us in our pubs, danced with us or took our girls to the cinema and went away to strike terror in our enemies in the far corners of the earth.'

The following week's Weston-super-Mare Gazette then carried a lengthy letter debunking the paper's presentation of life at Locking substituting a very grim version. The anonymous airman's letter alleged that certain huts were prepared as show pieces and that the guides kept the visitors away from the huts where 34 men were herded together, that the cinema showed pre-war films (when the projector was not broken), that the food was dreadful and that the delivery of mail left a lot to be desired.

The controversy continued with an article headed 'That place called Locking - is it Belsen or Paradise?' where an ex- corporal instructor was full of praise for the Station who looked back on his 16 months of No 5 SofTT as the happiest days of his life.

It is difficult to do justice to the scale of the wartime operation but the impressions are there: tens of thousands of people were trained, nearly 6,000 on parade at any one time, cooperation with the Royal Navy, the bombing raids and assistance given to the local people, that lecture on anti-gas procedures, and the 'At Home' day which lead to so much public argument.

Tales from the

Bob Collins, now living in Bridlington, remembers his time at RAF Locking well. In the latter part of 1938 he was at RAF Henlow being trained as a Flight Rigger having just completed a Fitter's Mate course at RAF Manston. He was in the Senior Entry and they were all surprised to learn that they were all to be detached to RAF Locking to open up the new Station.

'We arrived at Locking railway station (Milton Halt?) on 1 January 1939 and boarded a double-decker bus for the short journey to the Station. On arrival I was the first off the bus and into the camp gates, so was probably the first airman to arrive at RAF Locking.

We were billeted in wooden huts not far from the Guardroom (another wooden hut) and close to the cookhouse. The billet was next to open space which offered plenty of space for sport to work off surplus energy accrued from 16 weeks of rigorous training. Of interest is that next to the Guardroom was the Camp Tailor, a civilian, who would make any item of civilian clothing. This was useful as it must be remembered that on enlistment all items of civilian clothing were withdrawn and sent home. In our first year of Service personnel we were not allowed to wear civilian clothes. The Camp Tailor offered hire purchase terms and we could pay sixpence or a shilling a week depending on the cost of the purchase. Here I have a confession to make as I left RAF Locking owing a half crown, not an inconsiderable sum in those days when weekly pay was fourteen shillings, of which two shillings was held back to pay for any items of additional service clothing purchased form clothing stores. Luckily half a crown would purchase four pints of beer, five Woodbines and a bag of fish and chips, so we considered we were well off.

On that first visit I stayed at RAF Locking for about a month and experienced great kindness and friendship from the people of Weston with invitations at weekends to have tea at their houses. I well remember being invited, with a friend called Jones, to a

8 Over and Out

Tales from the 'Old Boys'

Methodist Minister's house. On the way in the bus, Jones and I discussed films and particularly a comic film star called Robertson Hare, who stood about five feet eight inches tall, long faced, horned rimmed glasses and bald head whose favourite expression was 'my little chic a dee'. On arrival at the Minister's house, who should answer the door but the spitting image of Robertson Hare?! I must admit that Jones and I could not stop ourselves from laughing and our host must have thought us extremely rude. However, our eventual explanation also amused the Minister and it served to break the ice and we spent many happy hours with him and his wife.

After this first visit we all returned to RAF Henlow, but only for a month, since our training was to be continued at RAF Locking, from where we graduated as Flight Riggers in July 1939.

Basic

During our training the facilities were, to say the least, basic. We didn't quite stand on each other's shoulders to rig the one and only aircraft, a Wapiti, but nearly so. Our instructors were not academically qualified, as they would be today, but nevertheless their practical approach stood us in good stead later on. Trammelling the box fuselage for fabric repairs would be alien to modern tradesman. During the course casual mention was made of hydraulics and we wondered why and what for! We were introduced to the theory of flight and I often chuckle when I play Bette Midler's 'Wind beneath my Wings' and wonder if anyone told her that it is the depression in the wing surface that gives the lift!

Finally, I recall the Flight Sergeant Pilot, who was i/c the course. If you were lucky, and had not been detailed on a Wednesday afternoon, he would take us for a never-to-be- forgotten trip in a Magister from Weston airfield. He would put the aircraft through all the acrobatic manoeuvres and, viewing this, you would thank your lucky stars someone else was the passenger, until it came to your turn. I can't recall anyone asking for a second helping.'

In June 1940, in addition to the trainees, the Station had also to accommodate several hundred men evacuated from Dunkirk.

Ex Sergeant 616361 L Huxley was also trained at RAF Locking in the very early years.

'I was posted as 'rookie' AC2 for training as a flight mechanic (Airframes) at a rate of pay of three shillings and sixpence per day, in accordance with the F434 which I still have, eventually passing out as a flight rigger with a pay increase of a shilling a day.

We were accommodated at the bottom of the camp in wooden huts (now 8 Area) and ate in a wooden Mess. I recall that the food was good, breakfast was porridge or grapefruit followed by eggs and bacon and tea from a communal urn. Occasionally there were prunes to start and kidneys on toast. For training we sat on our tool boxes for the academics and learnt our practical skills on either a Tiger Moth or Hawker Hart. At that time we received some musical instruments and I became a drummer boy in what was the first band on the Station. Off duty, it was a fourpenny bus ride to Weston where we were welcomed with open arms. The high spot was a visit to the 'Hole in the Wall', a well known bar for 'erks', where three pints of rough cider at fourpence a pint had us singing all the way back to camp to book in at the Guardroom by 10.30pm, or else 'jankers'! The 'Hole in the Wall' is gone, but was situated immediately behind the Floral Clock where now there are offices (McPherson and Partners?).'

On 16 October 1940 a Hurricane crashed at Chewton Mendip and the Polish pilot was admitted to the Station hospital. On its way to the crash site the Station crash guard happened upon a crashed Dornier which had lain unfound for several days with all the crew dead.

Tales from the 'Old Boys'

AC2 Flight Mechanics - Gerry Francis, Ron Cox and Les Boot

649383 AC2 Boot LN was trained as a flight mechanic from September 1939 to February 1940. Unfortunately his memories are not recorded but here are a selection of photographs given to the Station in 1997.

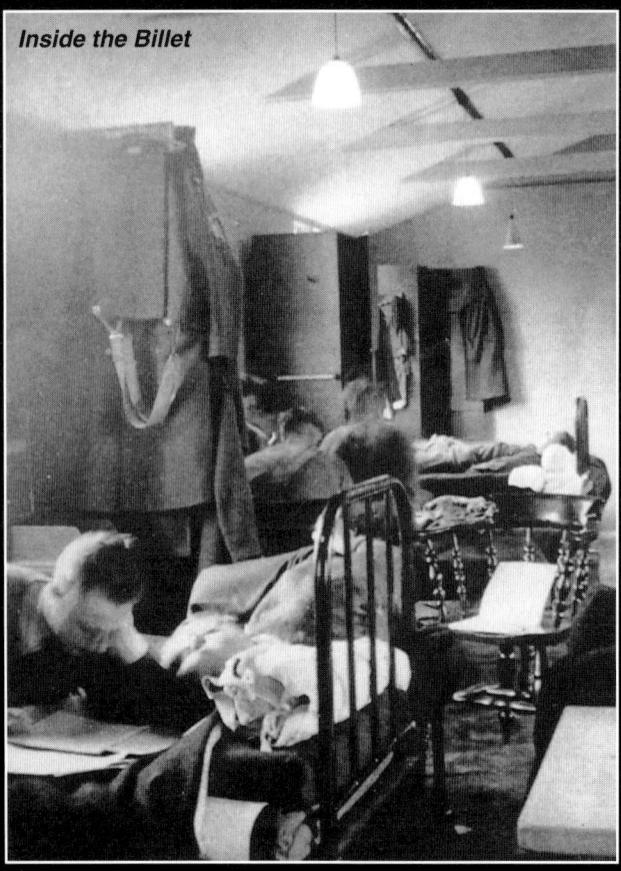

Inside the Billet

Hut Entry in No 2 Wing

Keeping up to Date

Camp Guard outside the Billets

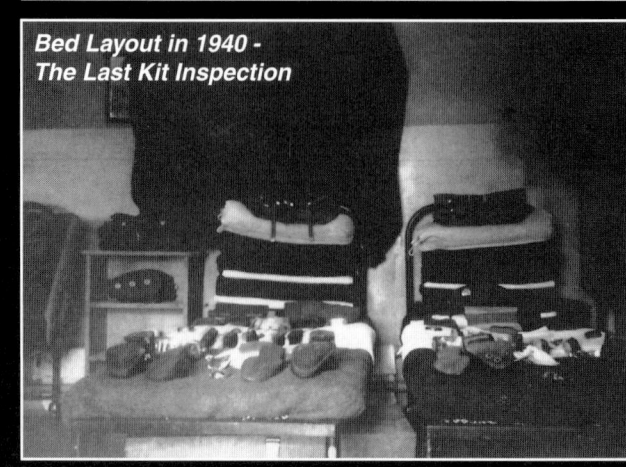

Bed Layout in 1940 - The Last Kit Inspection

10   Over and Out

Tales from the 'Old Boys'

Len Fisher, now living in Dorset, arrived at RAF Locking in 1941 and recalls:

'It was Spring 1941 and we had just finished our square bashing and had learnt a few new meanings for the word discipline. Myself and my compatriots were posted to RAF Locking Technical Training Wing for training as Flight Mechanics.

The camp was bursting at the seams and we were billeted in bell tents pitched near the perimeter. Shortly after settling in we were instructed through Daily Routine Orders to parade at 1000 hrs on the Saturday morning to hand in our service issue Jack Knives. No receipts were to be given as the knives would in future only be issued to those proceeding overseas.

My pal, a cockney called Ossie Fowler, thought that this was unfair so we decided that we would lay low on the Saturday morning and hide in the kit stacked around the centre pole of the tent. Three lads in the next tent decided to do the same but they weren't quiet enough and were discovered by the Corporal. We heard him yelling at them shouting that disciplinary action would be taken and we heard them being marched away their boots crunching on the gravel path. There was short silence immediately followed by a volley of 303 rifle fire from the adjacent range. Ossie turned to me and said, 'blimey Len, for three lousy pen knives they've shot em!'

I spent 16 weeks with Ossie - the length of the Flight Mechanics Course and then we parted never to meet again. I do recall Ossie telling me a story over a drink in the NAAFI the significance of which all servicemen will recognise. On joining up there was virtually no privacy and medical examinations were conducted behind partitioned hessian screens. One of these areas was the demesne of the ear doctor. The doctor whispered in both of Ossie's ears and received the traditional response - pardon. The doctor injected some fluid in both ears and told Ossie to return at 1430 hrs. When he returned he was seated opposite a small table and the doctor placed a white cloth and a kidney bowl on Ossie's shoulder. After which he proceeded to probe each ear in turn removing the contents into the bowl. When he had finished the doctor placed the bowl, covered with cloth, on the table. During the ensuing conversation the cloth slipped off the bowl to reveal the not inconsiderable contents (there was no way of telling how many patients the doctor had seen that afternoon). On seeing the mountain of wax Ossie gasped, 'Strewth Doc, no wonder I couldn't hear.' Even the staid doctor could not control the grin on his face.'

Roy Schofield who lives locally was a trainee in 1941, he recalls:

'Having done our square bashing on the promenade at Weston where we were in civilian billets and our HQ was in the Beach Hotel, we were moved to RAF Locking on 7 March 1941 to train as Flight Mechanics (Airframe) on a 16 week course.

Our accommodation was a wooden hut holding 28 airmen - C18, B Squadron, C Wing. Reveille - 0615 hrs, Breakfast 0700 hrs followed by a parade on the square at 0745 hrs; Lights Out 2215 hrs. Every morning and lunch time the camp Pipe and Drum Band escorted us to and from the workshops.

Church Parades were held every Sunday during which the order was given 'Catholics and Jews Fall Out'. These parades were also an opportunity for a certain element of the Fleet Air Arm to skive. Their ploy was for one of their number to 'faint on parade' whereupon their mates on either side would pick up the ailing matelot and carry him back to his hut, never to be seen again.

The cinema was the focal point of social activity but to visit you had to collect a pass from the picket hut and sign the book and then report back to return the pass after the film. Extra duties included fire picket, which lasted a week during which you were confined to camp and cook house duties which included cleaning the dining hall; at the time there were about 28 men to a table for meals.

After duty we were allowed into Weston,

Tales from the 'Old Boys'

Flight Mechanics returning for Fitter Training July 1941

travelling by bus from the camp gates. The last bus home was not very late in the evening so if you missed it there was a long walk home; I walked many a night!

There was the official camp laundry, which managed to often return the wrong items, and the Chinese Laundry, which we all patronised, called 'Chinky Woos'. I still recall the prices for cleaning:
Shirt - 41/2d
Collars (2) - 41/2d
Towel - 21/2d
Underpants - 2d
Vest - 2d
Handkerchief - 1d
Pr Socks - 21/2d

I also remember helping to build a sand bagged shelter for the CO. We needed to find a support for the roof on which to pile sand bags and managed to find an old crashed aircraft, from which we cut one of the wings in half.

Hut cleaning was a necessary chore and had to be completed satisfactorily before being allowed off camp. On one occasion we were placed third in order of merit because a chair had been placed in the storeroom outside instead of being in the hut and our gas capes were hung on the wall instead of being placed on the beds. For that, everyone's weekend passes were cancelled, except for those people who were in the winning hut. Occasionally it was necessary to get off camp quickly before you had time to clear your bed space. In such circumstances your duties were carried out by one of your room mates, to whom you had to return the favour, such was the spirit of camaraderie in the huts in those days.'

Pictured left: Trainees, including Roy Schofield, in March 1941 Hut C18, B Squadron, 3 Wing

12   *Over and Out*

Tales from the 'Old Boys'

Ernest Read (AC2 1765063) arrived at RAF Locking during the Summer of 1942 as an 18 year old to Class 5, Entry 164 to be trained as a Flight Mechanic Engines. He recalls that half the class was Fleet Air Arm, the standard practice of the time, and together they worked out that if they passed all the stage tests and didn't get recoursed they would graduate just before Christmas and get leave, for the first time since joining, at home.

Matelots Ashore in Weston

'Every 'erk' who did this course will remember the two weeks basic, the incessant filing, the angles for sharpening a drill bit and the alphabetic code for bolt sizes. We also learnt the intricacies of the Claudel Hobson carburetter and how to tune a Gypsy Major engine and who will forget the Volkes Oil Filter, where the oil goes from the outside to the inside in the outside filter and from the inside to the outside of the inside filter, or was it the other way round? I know I got it right at the trade test board. The final two weeks was 'Airfield Procedure' which aimed to give the trainee some experience of real squadron life. Oh deep joy, I was at last going to work on real aircraft. Parked all around the aprons to the hangar were various aircraft which were chocked behind wooden barriers to stop people walking into a rotating prop. The class was split into threes and we were instructed in turn to start the engine, run it at various speeds and carry out the Daily Inspection, while the other two men were to stand on the wings either side of the cockpit to observe. At last it was my turn, with a mixture of excitement and apprehension I slid down the cockpit and proceeded. 'Hells Bells!' What an experience, what with the roar of the engine and the rattles and bumps the aircraft seemed to be jumping about all over the place. Getting more and more scared I tried to grip the control column, but the more I tried the more the aircraft moved, eventually I throttled back and stopped the engine, feeling quite pleased with myself.

What I didn't expect was the reception I received from a group of very irate NCOs. What the 'blankety blank' did I think I was playing at - didn't I know that 'waggling the stick' was the recognised way of alerting everyone around of imminent danger?

It was obvious from the ground that with the aircraft at full throttle and threatening to jump the chocks there was a great danger of the aircraft careering across the apron and crashing into the hangar. While I was in the cockpit it was panic outside, the barriers had been removed and all the surrounding area, including the hangar, had been evacuated. What had gone wrong? The Fairy Battle engine was fitted with a boost override for emergency extra power in combat, with mis-operation constrained by a soft wire on the throttle lever. Whether a previous trainee had broken the wire I don't know, but its absence allowed me to push the throttle right through the gate straight into emergency combat power.

As I said we shared the course with the matelots who were billeted in their own Wing and followed Naval discipline. This amused us particularly when we went to town. After duty we donned 'best blue' as was the custom and sauntered out of the camp to catch the bus, not so the Navy lads, they had to wait at the Guardroom for the 'Liberty Boat' (a 3 Tonner) to take them ashore, with the same occurring for the return journey. If we saw the 3 Tonner passing we would all jump off the kerb and shout 'splash' loudly to make them feel at home.

In my time the food was of extremely variable quality. This was because the WAAF trainee cooks also did their three to four weeks training at RAF Locking and we could always tell when there was a new entry by the terrible concoctions served in the Mess. The quality then gradually improved until quite a high standard was reached until the dreaded day when that entry departed and a new one started.'

Tales from the 'Old Boys'

On 28 December 1941 a Whitley Mk 4 which had been bound for Gibraltar crashed on Weston Airfield. The crash guard had to move swiftly to recover the thousands of pounds in the aircraft and move it to safe keeping on the Station.

It is recorded that the Station rendered great assistance to the town during the air raids of the 27/28 June 1942 'by excavating the dead and injured and by dealing with the hundreds of incendiaries'.

In October 1942 Doug Williams arrived for training as Flight Mechanic (Engines) from his square bashing at Skegness.

'I well remembered standing in a squad waiting to be directed to various huts by the NCO in charge when a rather morose looking Leading Aircraftman passed by the rear rank with his forage cap perched precariously just above his right ear. In a scarcely audible voice he muttered 'Gas Squad' to no one in particular and vanished. At that moment volunteers were required for the Gas Contamination Hut and after consulting with two friends some sixth sense prompted me to put my hand up. It was a decision I never regretted - no guard duties, just a requirement to be available during Air Raid Warnings. I once had to leave the cinema in town after a 'screen flash' and got back to camp after passing the band playing in the drill hall on the Locking Road. The Leading Aircraftman, by the way, was the senior bod in the hut and we all had to cover for him whenever he was absent visiting his WAAF girlfriend on a balloon site. Once during a Civil Defence exercise we were required to play casualties and were left 'injured' outside a pub. By the time we were attended to we were slightly the worse for wear because of the frequent hospitality of the landlord.

Also during my time I had the unfortunate experience of being questioned for a murder on a bombsite. A RAF greatcoat button had been found at the scene and I had lost one that evening without realising it. Eventually I discovered that a Fleet Air Arm trainee had been arrested after killing a man who had spied on him while he was courting.

We were a mixed bunch with many talents, a friend of mine was a brilliant pianist which came in very useful when we visited a country pub. The locals took to us and plied us with drinks whenever we played - that was my first and last introduction to scrumpy. The Guardroom told us after that we had been delivered back to camp in a pony and trap, fortunately it was a holiday weekend and nothing more was said.'

Harold Skane, who lives in Weston, retired as Deputy Headteacher of Banwell Primary School after a lifetime of teaching, was at RAF Locking for two periods during the war years. In 1940 he was trained as a flight mechanic and having passed out with good marks was moved to Halton at the end of 1940 for further training as a Fitter 2e (engines) and returned to RAF Locking as an instructor.

He recalls teaching engine installation in the Bellman Hangar complex and De Havilland and Rotol propellers and general engineering. As an aside he believes that he was probably in the photograph of engine training in one of the hangars (now a 'T Block') because he recognises some of his contemporaries.

'As a Corporal I also ran the Station Music Club with 78 records, one day part way through a lesson someone sent a message to say that I had to go and see the CO

Cpl Skane second from left in 1942.

The Engine Shop

immediately - Gp Capt Paish. I dashed off thinking that I had committed some heinous blunder but when I arrived the CO wanted me to listen to his latest copy of Tchaikovsky's Piano Concerto No 1 and also to look at some new special equipment which played the music without any needle touching the record. What was I to say when I thought the recording was poor? Needless to say my colleagues thought I was creeping.

On 6 April 1942 at 1300 hrs, I and a friend were returning from the canteen situated on the 'D' carrying our irons and mug when we saw a Hampden aircraft flying very low towards Banwell across Locking village. As we watched, the aircraft seemed to pitch up and stall and turn towards the camp. It flew over the eastern side of the Station and crashed roughly where the Boilerhouse is now. We ran towards the crash to help and when we arrived saw that the pilot had been thrown clear and was on fire, I cut the leather jacket off him with a bone handled knife that I had, but I thought he was already dead. The other three members of the crew were also thrown clear. By that time medical help had arrived and corrugated iron fencing from the camp boundary was used for stretchers. All the crew were in fact killed. Later I found out that the Hampden was from I 6 OTU Upper Heyford and the pilot was a Canadian FS Allan McKeith (23 yrs old the same age as myself at the time) - the pilot and co-pilot are buried in the Commonwealth Graves Area of Weston Cemetery.

Many years later I felt that I should try and

FS McKeith's Grave in Weston

Tales from the 'Old Boys'

contact his family and after much research have corresponded with Sandy Lillwall (nee McKeith) second cousin of Allan and I have shown his grave to members of his family. (Recorded at the Air Historical Branch Aircraft Loss Card is that the aircraft carried 4x250lb live bombs which fortunately did not explode).

'I enjoyed racket sports and at the time was keen on Table Tennis. The table, I recall, was placed on a highly polished floor which made the game impossible to play, so I got a bucket of boiling hot water and cleaned the polish of the floor. For this I was charged and brought before the adjutant for damaging property.'

When I was an instructor in late 1943 there was an experiment to release RAF tradesmen for more active service by training WAAFs as flight mechanics. We were sent to help lift the tail of a Blenheim onto a trestle to allow the riggers to do their checks as part of their training. When we got there, much to our surprise, we were unable to lift the tail, mystified we investigated and soon found out why. Right at the rear of the aircraft in a very tight space we found two airmen snogging with two WAAFs! We had many meetings on the subject of WAAFs and engineering and some would say they were not natural mechanics.

Sport was an abiding pastime and while I was at RAF Locking Joe Louis gave a demonstration of boxing and Frank Soo, an international footballer from Stoke City, played for the Station. I enjoyed racket sports and at the time was keen on Table Tennis. The table, I recall, was placed on a highly polished floor which made the game impossible to play, so I got a bucket of boiling hot water and cleaned the polish off the floor. For this I was charged and brought before the adjutant for damaging property. Although sympathetic to my tale, he was not that sympathetic, and I was reprimanded and warned to follow the standard procedure in future, a course of action which I had already tried and which had failed.

We used current aircraft for training and I recall the Typhoon with its Napier 24 cylinder H engine - four banks of six cylinders, two sets of which were inverted (48 spark plugs to change) which was parked by the Bellman hangars. This beast was very powerful to run up and hold back on full throttle. Also a Lysander which as a type had a tendency to backfire. One day when I was running it up, it typically backfired into the carburettor which promptly caught fire, I stood up and called for help to extinguish the fire but instead of the foam being directed at the engine it was directed at me; I got covered with foam and the fire carried on burning.

As a Corporal we had some less pleasant duties to perform, one was Bus Duty where we had to go the Bus Station and gather all the airmen together for the last bus and get them back to camp, most of whom were somewhat worse for wear. We also had to meet the trains at Milton Halt and march the returning airmen back to camp along the dark Locking Moor Road.

Talking of drink, many airmen had their first taste of cider while they were under training. Some people seem to get very quiet after a drink or two while others become noisy. I recall one chap, who was over six feet tall, having had an evening on cider returning to camp in a 'noisy' condition; he was so strong it took five of us to hold him down and we had to tie him to the bed to keep him quiet.'

WAAF Trophies for Best Hut and Best Hut Garden in 1942

Tales from the 'Old Boys'

Rex Austin was trained as an engine mechanic in 1943/44 and his first impression of RAF Locking was that it did not seem to be a bad place at all, well set out among really nice country.

Rex Austin with 221 Entry Class 1E in 1943

'The huts were standard RAF type with a large hot water pipe running behind the beds which came in very handy to put one's clothes on for a warm start to the day. There was a covered walkway to the ablutions and, providing you got up smartly at reveille, hot water. If you turned up late the water might well have cooled off. Reveille was a bugle call over the tannoy system, as was lights out, which meant just that, as they were switched off from the master switch at the end of the row of huts.

I arrived on 16 September 1943 and was told that No 221 Entry would not start until the 24th, any hope of a week's skiving was soon dashed as we would all be on fatigues for most of the time. In fact the very next day we were detailed for guard duty at the crash site of a Miles Martinet target tug which had crashed on the marshes off Brean Down. I well remember collecting rations and a tent and making our way to a very bleak landscape where the night was bright moonlight and cold, sitting in the cockpit of the aeroplane to keep warm. I also spent time on fire piques which entailed sleeping in the Fire Piquet Hut located near the cinema. As part of that duty we took turns to be on duty in the cinema - free admission.

My course started on the Friday and we were 'fell in' at the top of the hill and marched down to the workshops, overalls under our left arm and led by the Bugle Band. The first part of the course was Basics - use of tools and shaping a block of metal then on to Prelim Engines. The highlight of the course, apart from the 48 hour pass, was instruction on the starting and running of the resident Hurricane, Spitfire, Blenheim and Beaufighter; I remember being very disappointed that I missed out on the latter. There was also a Blackburn Botha which, if it could be started, breathed fire and smoke like a dragon.

In those days nearly everyone smoked and, as smoking was not allowed in the workshops, there were frequent requests to visit the latrines, so in order to keep a check on things one would have to take a token, usually an engine part - crank rod, piston or whatever. On arrival at the latrines one would be met by a wall of fug and nearly have enough engine

parts to construct an engine!

Life was not all academic as there were sports afternoons. On the first afternoon I was not sure what to go for, my mind was soon decided for me - rugby. Being eight and a half stone and five feet three inches, I made sure that on the following weeks I went on the cross country, where I got out of camp into nice countryside with the added bonus that, if you did not hang about, you could return early and be first in the queue for the cookhouse.

A 48 hour pass in November was more than welcome and we were marched down to the railway halt and on return, nearly midnight,

Over and Out 17

Tales from the 'Old Boys'

were met by NCOs with torches to escort us back to camp. Some Sunday evenings I would go to the Methodist Church in Weston when, after the service, there would be a an enjoyable social hour. As a result of this, at Christmas we were invited out but had to turn the offers down because of transport difficulties. On camp there was the occasional NAAFI dance and ENSA put on some quite good shows. CO's parade was once a month, hut inspection was weekly after the domestic night and I recall one lad being charged because some dust had been discovered between the bars of the bedhead!

At Christmas 1943 there were three days off and my diary records that the dinner was 'smashing' and that there was a football match between the WAAFs and the Sergeants and to end the day a grand dance in No 3 Workshop, the band being none other than Harry Roy's Ragamuffins; and I got to bed at 2am.

As the course came to an end there was a week of revision followed by the dreaded board. I did pass but not as well as I had hoped - a really good pass mark would have meant going on to a Fitters Course at RAF Cosford. We finished the course on the Friday and on the following Wednesday paraded for our postings, as we dismissed there was a chorus of where's this airfield, this MU, or in my case where is RAF Chivenor? - our geography was woeful. And so loaded onto buses it was seven days leave and on to 172 Squadron at RAF Chivenor.'

This is a small ditty from the period:

I'm an FME
Just a poor U/T
But before I'm done
I'll be an AC1
I've done my Basics and Prelims
Church parades and sung the hymns
Mags and carbs I did with ease
My NCOs I tried to please
My Gen Book now is getting full
Despite the hardships and the bull
Fourteen more weeks I have to go
Before I've finished here
and then its leave and home to go

Anon

Prior to D Day the Station provided supervision for range firing on the Brean Sands range and it is recorded in the ORB that on the 22 April 1944 260 American Army personnel received range practice.

In 1944 Mr Pearn, now living in Oakdale Gardens in Worle, was the Flight Sergeant policeman in charge of the military police.

'The Guardroom was of wooden construction in the same position as it is now, but the gate was narrower. The Armoury was opposite the Guardroom and the SHQ faced the gate on the 'D'. RAF Locking was then home to a training establishment 5 SofTT but also parented Weston Airfield. Also at the first left turn off the road down towards the BAJ Factory (right off the Locking Moor Road) there was another hutted camp for Polish WAAF who were employed at various locations on the camp. One interesting thing was that when Weston was bombed the RAF firetender based on Weston airfield was the first on the scene.

The main road leading to the new training blocks was named after Gp Capt McCrea who was the first Station Commander of RAF Locking. During my time he was the Commanding Officer of the recruit unit based on Weston sea front. Parks Road was named after WO Parks, who was the Apprentice Wing Discip WO and Leadham Road Came from Sqn Ldr Leadham who was an Admin Officer.

I was posted from RAF Locking in November 1945, so I was only on camp for a year, most of that time was spent looking for accommodation for my wife and family as there were no married quarters on the Station. During that time RAF Locking was always accepted as being part of Weston and we were all treated with respect and made most welcome in the town.'

Tales from the 'Old Boys'

- July 1945 saw the move of the Polish Technical Training School away from RAF Locking to RAF Cammeringham.
- Italian Cooperators (POWs) were withdrawn in February 1946 and it is recorded in the ORB that in the main they were good workers and their services would be missed.
- On 12 November 1946 a DH Hornet crashed at Charterhouse and the Station provided the now standard crash site guard.

Mr Newland now living in Byfleet was trained at RAF Locking in the immediate post war years as a Fitter Airframes:

'My first visit to RAF Locking was as an ATC cadet on a summer camp in 1944. We had an air experience flight in an Airspeed Oxford from Weston Airfield and lessons in the Workshop Hangars on camp. The instructional airframes were mostly the long nosed Blenheim and Oxfords and there were an assortment of radial and liquid cooled engines.

I joined the RAF as a regular in 1946 and after initial training was posted to RAF St Athan - No 4 SofTT to be trained as a Flight Mechanic Airframes, thereafter I was moved to No 54 MU Newmarket before returning to RAF Locking as AC1 3500114 to receive training as a Fitter 2 Airframes, a Group 1 Trade.

The Double Decker Bus

The Crashed Boston Aircraft

I arrived at RAF Locking in the evening of one of the blackest days of the Station's history, when a number of trainees going on leave were accidentally killed when a Boston Mk 3 aircraft AL 467 undershot and collided with the top of their double decker bus as it crossed the end of the runway on the Locking Moor Road. Eight airmen were killed and eleven injured, some seriously.

View Along Locking Moor Road Towards Weston

Over and Out 19

Tales from the 'Old Boys'

Our course also included members of the Norwegian Air Force.

Training was carried out on Typhoon, Mosquito and Oxford airframes in the large unheated workshops which, during the bad winter of 46/47, were like refrigerators. A heavy blanket of snow covered the camp for many weeks and at one time the Station was cut off from Weston by severe drifting between the two bridges over the railway. Due to the severe weather, numerous RAF stations were temporarily closed down, but it was decided by higher authority that RAF Locking would remain open as long as possible. Parades were reduced to a minimum and, due to frozen pipes and lack of heating and hot water, inspections were curtailed and many weekend passes granted.

On one occasion the trains returning from Bristol were delayed for several hours. Just prior to the departure of the train from Bristol the Tannoy announced that the train would stop at Milton Halt for RAF Locking personnel as there would be no buses available at the main station. The walk from Milton Halt to the camp was through drifts several feet deep so we were all pretty cold and wet when we eventually arrived. As the weather improved and a steady thaw set in the nightly fire piquet became a burst pipe patrol and a large number of leaks were discovered.

With the spring came the Trade Test Board and as a newly qualified AC1 Fitter Airframes I left RAF Locking for the last time. Looking back my stay had been both enjoyable and eventful.'

From April to July 1947 200 German POWs were held in the hutted encampment located where the Knightcott Industrial Estate is now. In July 1987 Richard Knoele and his wife revisited the place where he was held prisoner.

John Dunn, who has lived in Weston for 44 years, 2237446, it's an aircrew number, entered the RAF initially in 1941 but was subsequently released for war work as a setter - operator for shell fuses. In 1946 he was called up:

'After square bashing and holding camps I was posted to RAF Locking for training as a Group 1 Air Fitter (two courses). We were in billets - six abreast near the Locking Road.

At dinner an officer and sergeant cook would ask whether there were any complaints. One officer would always bring his dog - an Alsation and on one particular day there were complaints about the meat in the stew. The officer asked the complainant for his fork, skewered a piece of meat and threw it to the floor for the dog and said, 'if it's good enough for the dog it's good enough for you!' We heard later that the officer had been reprimanded.

About 40 West Indians ate by themselves at the end of the Mess Hall and they had their own cook. One day one of them was chased through the Mess by the cook with his chef's knife - he's probably still running.

There were times when I was given 'jankers' for lateness or sleeping in lectures. It was always three days or seven days reporting to the Guardroom at 6am and 5pm for punishment duties, mainly in the cookhouse washing pots and pans. There were compensations as it was always warm and there were titbits.

1946/47 was the coldest winter on record and there was a shortage of coke, so everyone had to play their part in finding fuel of any kind for the fire. At work we sat in our greatcoats, there was no heating in the hangars, and once or twice during each period we would form up

> *'At dinner an officer and sergeant cook would ask whether there were any complaints. One officer would always bring his dog - an Alsation, and on one particular day there were complaints about the meat in the stew. The officer asked the complainant for his fork, skewered a piece of meat and threw it to the floor for the dog and said, "if it's good enough for the dog, it's good enough for you."'!*

Tales from the 'Old Boys'

Taken in 1948 - Note the aircraft behind the Bellman Hangars, a Lancaster and Mosquito can be just seen

outside and run around the hangar to get warm. In addition we were given hot tea and extra leave.

On one occasion it was reported that someone on the flight knew where a deserter from the flight was living. We were lined up 120 strong outside the flight office in the rain with the Warrant Officer questioning us about the missing man. To our surprise along came a corporation dust cart, the driver of which was an ex 8th Army man who didn't take kindly to being asked to go the other way round. He and the Warrant Officer exchanged 'pleasantries' when the adjutant arrived to talk the driver and we were dismissed back to the billets out of the way of the dust cart.

I recall hitching a lift back from Weston at the bottom of Locking Road. A black van stopped, the driver was going to Twickenham, but he could give us a lift provided we could sit on the shelves in the back. We got in, he shut the doors and drove off; as he started he said 'don't worry about the man in the coffin - he's dead'.

When we were due for 48 hour leave we had to line up in flights for the double decker buses to take us to the station. The Flight Sergeant would decide which bus you travelled on. One particular leave we returned to camp to find out that an aircraft with its undercarriage down had taken the top off one of our double decker buses.

Sometimes when returning to camp I ended up catching a later train making me late in reporting. Some of us used to get out of the opposite side of the train, cross the railway lines and race across the fields to camp to avoid getting into trouble.'

On 18 September 1948 the Station hosted an 'At Home Day' to commemorate the 'Battle of Britain'.

Over and Out 21

Finally, from the wartime period:

The Flight Mechanics Moan

The lords of the air they call us
They speak of our growing Fame
The front page in every paper
Is adorned with some pilot's name

Connected with deeds of valour
Performed azure blue
With Messerschmitt, Heinkel and Dornier
Flaming to earth in two

But there is one bloke you never hear mentioned
You never hear his name
He doesn't fly in a clear blue sky
Or pose for the press in a plane

His job isn't what you would call romantic
And he is not in the public eye
But the hero can't be without him
And I will tell you the reason why

He runs up the kite each morning
He fills up the tank each night
He sees that the engine is running sweetly
And the oil pressure is kept just right

He's out in the field each morning
He's out there as twilight fades
Pulling his weight to keep the kite
Ready to go on the raids

The next time you read your paper
With photos of smiling crews
Remember the bloke you didn't see
Although he's only an AC2

So next time you cheer the pilot
As the enemy falls a wreck
Remember the bloke you don't see
Yours truly, a humble flight mech

Lou Lewis, 1920538

The local community

1950 saw the start of the transfer of No 1 Radio School from RAF Cranwell. Wireless and radar fitter airmen trainees and radio apprentices were on the move to the South West. The phased transfer was mainly of RAF personnel and was completed in 1952. There were, however, a substantial number of civilian instructional staff who were abandoning a considerable portion of their history in Lincolnshire, at a time when they were approaching the twilight of their working lives. They were about to begin a widely different existence; even the climatic change was going to take some getting used to.

The impact of these transfers was also to be quite far reaching for the villagers of Locking. The urgent housing needs of the newcomers were only partially met by the housing agencies in and around Weston. The shortfall was addressed by some taking up temporary board and lodgings; others were able to rent from RAF Locking; including temporary married quarters situated in Hillend, Banwell. A few were more enterprising and ambitious and designed and built interesting properties in the town.

Redundant

At about the same time the Gloucester Aircraft Manufacturing Company was reducing production levels and quite a number of technical staff were being made redundant and relocated to Westland Helicopters on Weston Airfield and Bristol Aerojet in Hutton.

The local rural district council responsible for Locking was Axbridge. The housing department there were persuaded by the RAF to build a fairly large estate in Locking Village. The responsibility for allocating these houses to civilian instructional staff rested with RAF Locking. Although they were built reasonably quickly, the majority of the ex- Cranwell staff had been housed by the time the properties became available in 1957. However, there was no shortage of takers because a shortfall in instructors on transfer led to an influx of new staff and these, together with the Gloucester

(From an article by Bill Larder)

contingent, welcomed the houses with open arms even though the rents were set at an economic level. Thus the nucleus of a community was born, mainly youngsters bound together by similar needs and one or two oldsters there to moderate any outrageous behaviour.

Invaders

Before the new build, Locking Village was a tiny picturesque, rose covered Somerset village. The Post Office was a hole in the wall affair and the local residents did not want their somnolent existence to be rudely awakened by 'foreign' invaders who wanted upheaval. First of all a pub, then garbage collection and a modern sewage system. The impact on the old community was quite dramatic.

Parish Council meetings in the Church Hall were extremely well attended; often bursting at the seams. It wasn't long before street lighting appeared - the cost a 1d increase on the rates. It took a lot of glib talking and haranguing to get this. Then a liquor licence was extracted for a Proprietary Club opened in 1959 to be run in the Manor House by its new owner, a former Squadron Leader.

The majority of the members were incomers and it wasn't long before the land adjoining the Manor House was sold for building 15 chalet type houses which sold for £4,000 each in 1961/62. The Post Office was moved into a shop introduced by the Axbridge initiative and the mains sewage system eventually materialised together with a fortnightly rubbish collection.

(Note that the Coach House Inn is a recent addition to the Locking Village scene, although in part a very old building, it was originally the coach house for the Manor.)

While all this was happening No 1 Radio School was progressing and developing. It became obvious that both Service and civilian staff were going to be involved in the exploding electronics revolution and unless civilian qualifications were sought career prospects in the future would be bleak. Electronics training in Weston Technical College was almost non existent, so RAF Locking educational staff took over a section of the college to provide tuition to servicemen and civilians for City and Guilds technical training qualifications. This continued for several years until the College was able to set up its own organisation.

Although academic and trade training were the main aims of the Radio School, sporting activities and the fundamentals of leadership were never far behind. Apprentice sporting standards became the target for local civilian teams to aim at. Apprentices became renowned for their ability and sportsmanship and were well represented in local teams. They, in fact, gave considerable support to the organisation of local clubs who were in their infancy and quite inexperienced. Adult trainees and members of staff made their way into local teams for cricket, rugby and football and sportsmen from RAF Locking were often sought for representation for County competitions.

The building of the Manor Gardens estate by the Axbridge housing project lead to a mushrooming of new bungalows to the side. There was no shortage of buyers and the estate at Mendip Rise subsequently developed in 1965. The consequent increase in school age children also lead to the building, in 1965, of the Locking Village Primary School and the consequent closure of the school within the Camp boundary. The new primary school was still linked to the camp by a footbridge to provide safe access for RAF Locking children, who continued to be the

> 'Before the new build, Locking Village was a tiny, picturesque, rose covered Somerset village. The Post Office was a hole in the wall affair and the local residents did not want their somnolent existence to be rudely awakened by "foreign" invaders who wanted upheaval. First of all a pub, then garbage collection and a modern sewage system. The impact on the old community was quite dramatic.'

Over and Out 23

mainstay of the new school.

Of course, the Church Hall was by now much too small for parish meetings and a new hall was designed and built (1965), but not before another large estate was under way in the area of the Orchard, completed in 1967.

The RAF was pleased to make use of these to house some of their families while a further tranche of new married quarters were being built.

Profound effect

The move of the training school had a profound effect on the village and the villagers. Eventually, the Proprietary Club was closed and the license transferred, in 1963, to the new watering hole - The Coach House Inn, which was much enlarged from the original building.

The Post Office and adjoining shops, together with the playing fields, are still the focal point of village life and there is thriving village hall and very successful primary school.

Coach House Inn

**LOCKING VILLAGE
NR. WESTON-SUPER-MARE**

Telephone: Banwell 822506

SIT IN OUR OLDE WORLDE PUB
and enjoy REAL ALE, including
WHITBREAD BEST BITTER and
DRAUGHT BASS

Large range of SNACKS served
at all times

• CHILDREN'S ROOM   • PARKING FOR 100 CARS
Skittle Alley available for hire

Boy Entrants

**Teenage airmen 'hold the Key to Good Workmanship'
(reproduced from 'Review' - 1949)**

'Four hundred boys, many of them from the homes of serving airmen, are setting out this month to begin an Air Force career at RAF Locking, headquarters of the Boy Entrant Scheme. Early in 1951 they will emerge as skilled technicians for regular service, ready to take their places in the ground crews of the squadrons and to carry on the tradition of the men who kept the aircraft flying for the great battles of war.

Although the Boy Entrant Scheme has only been running for two years since its post war revival - it first started in 1934 - parents all over Britain and in many places abroad have been quick to realise the value of the training it offers.

Hundreds of boys between the ages of 15 and 17 and a half have taken advantage of the RAF's unique 'university' in order to benefit from the 18 months course which includes not only free technical training but general education as well.

The scheme is designed for those whose standard of education is not quite up to the School Certificate level demanded for RAF Halton's aircraft apprentices. For the 'Boys' there is no entrance examination - all they need is nomination by a local education authority, the Boy Scouts Association or other approved organisations, together with the ability to pass intelligence and aptitude tests at a selection board.

Successful candidates have their first taste of Air Force life at RAF Locking, home of No 5 SofTT, and one of the most pleasantly situated of all RAF camps set amid ideal country barely four miles from Weston-super-Mare.

This month, on the Station's extensive playing fields and in its comfortable barrack blocks and recreation rooms and its large modern workshops, 400 boys of the 8th Entry are starting their course. In less than two years they will have been transformed into qualified technicians, ready to tackle any job in their chosen trade.

Boy Entrants

Some, indeed, may have won RAF Cadetships by then, for all boys have an opportunity to compete for these scholarships which may lead to permanent commissions in the General Duties, Equipment or Secretarial Branches or in the RAF Regiment.

At present, Boy Entrants are restricted to the Group B trades of airframe, engine, instrument or armament mechanics, air and ground radio mechanics and telegraphists. Therefore, although every Boy Entrant starts off at RAF Locking, not all receive their trade training there.

Those selected as potential armament mechanics are transferred, after the two weeks 'settling in' period to No 10 SofTT at RAF Kirkham. Telegraphists go to No 3 RS at RAF Compton Basset, and air and ground radio mechanics to No 2 RS at RAF Yatesbury.

And they get paid while they train. For the first year, pay is at the rate of 1s 6d a day, increasing to 2s a day and up to 4s a day at 17 and a half.'

The following is a piece submitted by Peter Adams which tells the Boy Entrant story 1947-1950:

'It was hardly surprising that the initial civil reaction to the military decision to resurrect the pre-war RAF Boy Entrant scheme - barely a year after the end of the war - seemed to strengthen the opinion that 'them in power were incapable of applying anything other than traditional policies.' (The sort of policy which ensured that at the start of World War Two, the British Army was fully equipped with the best trenching tools developed during, and immediately following, World War One). However, subsequent history proved the wisdom of the 1946 decision in terms of the forward planning and preparation that was necessary to cope with the post-war turmoil of the Berlin Airlift; the campaign in Malaya and the war in Korea. Ironically, the military decision dovetailed neatly with the emerging civil needs of the immediate post-war era.

The demobilisation of war-time conscripted personnel was proceeding apace, but was creating resettlement and retraining problems for many civilian employers. One consequence was a pronounced deficit of training facilities and apprenticeships for young men ready to leave school, but not yet old enough to commence their National Service commitment. For such young men, the chance to receive a good aircraft engineering training, together with the provision of 'board and keep', was too good an opportunity to be missed. The initial response vindicated the merit of the military decision to reintroduce the RAF Boy Entrant scheme - a decision which had a significant influence on RAF recruitment for many years and which was to play an important role in the history of Royal Air Force Locking.

The induction process into the RAF Boy Entrant scheme commenced with locally held examinations at the end of 1946. Candidates were then called to attend for aptitude tests and a medical examination at RAF North Weald in the spring of 1947. In May of that year, some 370 newly recruited young men were moved in batches from North Weald, by train, to Weston-super-Mare. For many, it was their first experience of being away from home; and for all of us there was only a brief glimpse of Weston before we were transported to RAF Locking, where we would be 'turned into airmen' before being allowed out of camp again.

Kitting out

As was probably common at every military induction centre, the process of kitting out presented its fair share of problems. The trouble was, we young men came in all shapes and sizes; but it seemed that every Supplies & Procurement Officer in the RAF had assumed that this was his opportunity to transfer any slow moving and/or extreme size fitting stock. The majority of us probably took size 13 in detachable collars (six off to be issued to accompany the three off collarless shirts). The largest stock of collars held in the clothing store, was size 12! 'Take these for now you can change them later', was the storeman's standard response to almost any query. In most cases the ability to continue to breathe was achieved by making two small slits at the outer end of each front collar-stud hole and reinforcing the ends of these slits with needle and cotton. The latter being found in a most odd looking linen wallet known as a 'housewife'. Incidentally, we were never issued

Boy Entrants

with collar studs, these were available from NAAFI but not enough to go round, so for the unlucky ones a half-inch 2BA mushroom headed bolt and thin nut provided the only stop-gap.

There seemed to be no consideration given to apportioning the general issue clothing in relation to the size of the person being kitted out. 'Three of these - one on, one in the wash, and one for kit layout' became the stock phrase. I clearly remember a rather stocky - but not miniature - young man, who shall be identified only as 'BL', demonstrating his ability to tuck the legs of his 'underpants, woollen, short' into the tops of his 'socks, woollen, short' with complete ease, and remarking that 'it would be comfortable if we get another winter like last year' (1946/47). By contrast, 'Lofty H' - one of the tallest lads in the first entry - had a four inch gap, which exposed his navel, between the bottom of his 'vests woollen' and the top of his underpants.

To those of us who had thought of bed and bedding as being essentially for comfort, there was a certain disillusionment with the RAF drill-instructors interpretation. 'Three biscuits, one palliasse pillow, one palliasse case, five blankets, two sheets; the primary purpose of which is to enable a term geometric and stable base to be prepared, on which you will lay out your kit for inspection'. This was usually followed by the equally meaningless phrase 'beds will always be made up as laid down on the demonstration posters'. Gradually, with the aid of a stiff piece of cardboard, we developed the ability to fold our 'Greatcoats - airman for the use of', into the correct sized rectangle to expose the required two polished buttons to the front. Folded and stacked into our steel bedside lockers, they had a much more military appearance than when worn. Most, according to the drill NCO's, gave the wearer the 'appearance of pregnant penguins'.

> 'To those of us who had thought of bed and bedding as being essentially for comfort, there was a certain disillusionment with the RAF drill-instructors' interpretation.'

Probably the most abused part of our uniform was the peaked hat adorned with an orange and brown chequered band, which was worn as part of our 'best blue' and walking out dress. At that time, peaked hats were usually associated with guardsmen, RAF and military police and the Gestapo, and there was a determined effort to style one's hat along one of those lines. The 'conversion' followed one of two stages. The first stage was to insert a broken off hacksaw blade behind the deaf spring which supported the front of the hat. This made it much more upright and acceptable - until the time came when the hacksaw blade pierced through the material and poked out through the front crown. Stage two, involved the very careful cutting of the outer two inches of the stitching at both sides of the peak. This allowed the peak to swivel on the remaining three and a half inches of attachment stitching and be flattened down over the forehead, eyes and nose. This was real 'guardsman' style, and had the advantage that it permitted the peak to be in the regulation position for parades etc. but required only a press with the palm of the hand to take up the cavalier style. Eventually of course, the NCO's became aware of this practice, at about the same time as the remaining peak stitching became fatigued. They adopted a practice of checking 'hat on square' by grabbing the peak. Imagine, if you will, a number of airmen, who have already been classified as having the appearance of pregnant penguins, on parade and standing to attention, wearing orange and brown chequered, banded, peakless peaked, hats and looking rather like refugees from the Russian Navy. It was always good for at least another seven days 'jankers'!

To the majority of us, having graduated through the Air Training Corps or the School Cadet Force, the mandatory 'square bashing' didn't present any real problems. Nevertheless, we had our share of those who had difficulty in differentiating between left and right, and those who - while being able to walk with a perfectly normal gait - when required to march seem compelled to swing the right arm in unison with the right leg. We were considered proficient in the square bashing role, when we were able to 'form threes', 'advance in column of route and review order', 'cover the ground with some semblance of formation' - without kicking the heels of the man in front, 'halt in unison' - without giving the appearance of a train hitting the buffers and perform all the rifle drill movements without dropping the Lee Enfield, that was supposed to be 'our best friend'. At long last we were to be allowed out of camp.

'Civilians may walk; elderly civilians may stroll, but young fit airmen will MARCH - anywhere, everywhere and at all times'. Thus spake the Flight Sergeant (Discip) at the pep-talk which took place at the end of the Saturday morning parade, before we were allowed out of camp for the first time.

We had become well used to marching everywhere on the camp.

Down to the training hangars; to school; back to the Wing for lunch - we called it dinner in those days; back to the hangars for the afternoon session; back to the Wing for tea; and nearly always behind the Trumpet and Drum Band which had somehow mysteriously come into being during our first couple of weeks at RAF Locking. The band was undoubtedly militarily smart and added a fair

> 'Imagine, if you will, a number of airmen, who have already been classified as having the appearance of pregnant penguins, on parade and standing to attention, wearing orange and brown chequered, banded, peakless, peaked hats and looking rather like refugees from the Russian Navy.'

Food, Glorious Food

degree of gilding to our marching performance. The main short-fall was, perhaps, a rather limited repertoire. Two threes and a seven - and into 'Georgia' seemed to be 'top of the pops' for the first term of the first entry at RAF Locking. Sometimes it seemed that this was the only tune in the world - apart from 'reveille' first thing in the morning, and 'lights out'.

In reality, the Flight Sergeant (Discip's) warning was unnecessary. We were sufficiently proud of our brand new suits of RAF blue and the impressive chequered peak hats, that we walked tall (some might even say we swaggered) on our first safari into Weston-super-Mare. Fortunately, because it was early summer, we were not, at that time, required to wear our 'pregnant penguin' greatcoats. As I recollect, our first outing mainly consisted of promenading the Weston-super- Mare seafront, seeking out a local photographer - two head and shoulder prints at 3/6d - one for Mum and one for the girlfriend, ready in about two hours - another circuit of the town's amenities; round to the bus station and back to camp before they finished serving tea in the cookhouse. It would be wrong for us to claim that we were immediately and unreservedly accepted by the civil population. Perhaps this

Boy Entrants

was due to a rumour that we had come from Borstal remand homes. A rumour possibly started by the parents and civilian boyfriends of the young ladies of Weston, who were deemed to be at risk from this influx of young foreign blood. Happily, this reserve was very short-lived and, with increasing frequency, we were invited into the homes of the young ladies we met up with at weekends. I think we must still have been of an age when their matriarchs were ready to mother us - providing we accompanied them to church on Sundays! The confirmation that we had established an entente cordiale with the people of Weston-super-Mare, became apparent at the end of our first term at Locking, when we went on end-of-term leave. The platforms of the railway station were awash with the local young ladies - and many of their mothers - who had turned up to see us off. There was a similar scene some five weeks later when we returned to continue our training. By this time we felt like 'old hands', but this time domiciled among friends.

We quickly re-established familiarity with our hutted encampment, and re-adapted to the routine of service life - although, after lights out, the first couple of nights were marked by the telling, re-telling and embellishment of 'when I was on leave' stories. In the mornings, we awoke to the strident tone of the reveille trumpet, made a mad dash for the ablutions before all the hot water ran out; then off to the cookhouse before the porridge congealed or the marmalade ran out. After breakfast, bed-making, bedspace cleaning, final polishing of boots and buttons and we were ready for the first parade of the day. That is unless you were 'Room Orderly' - in which case you had another half hour of room cleaning!

One of our biggest problems would, today, be described as 'cash flow'. Although our pay was 10/- per week, we received only 10/- at fortnightly intervals. The remainder was held as 'credit', which was paid to us less deductions for barrack room damages etc. at the end of term when we went on leave. Although the concept was good, the reality was, to the majority a financial disaster. Ten shillings seldom stretched over the two week period, once one had purchased razor blades, shaving cream, soap, toothpaste, boot-polish, Brasso, writing paper, envelopes and stamps. These last three items being essential, because without them one could not write begging letters home requesting another sub, and, with any luck, perhaps another food parcel. Agreed, prices were not comparable with what they are today; but even NAAFI tea at 1d. a cup, an Eccles cake at 2d., and a seat at the camp cinema for 4d., made significant inroads into our financial status and encouraged the more enterprising to exploit the less affluent.

Prohibited

Although smoking was prohibited, unless you were over 17 and the holder of a smoking pass, cigarettes could easily be bought outside the camp, and sold off individually at a premium rate. Thereby emerged the 'Cigarette Barons'. None of us needed to smoke, but we indulged from time to time just for the sheer hell of it. To be caught smoking was good for seven days 'jankers' (confined to camp with extra duties) - usually in the 'tin room' in the cook-house. There was one particular corporal instructor who perfected the art of knocking on the door of a lavatory from which smoke was arising with the request 'have you got a light mate?' The desire to be helpful, lead to the downfall of many!

With the exception of one or two isolated instances, there was seldom any major grouse when one became a 'defaulter'. Being 'on jankers' was regarded as being a sort of occupational hazard. It didn't seem to imply any personal vindictiveness when you were dished out with so many days penalty. I can recall very few incidents where the punishment didn't seem to fit the crime. One did occur after we had actually passed out, and received our posting notices. One of our member had been hospitalised with vaccine fever, and so did not travel with the group to our new station. After being released from hospital he was retained at RAF Locking and excused duties while his posting arrangements were finalised. He was found in bed after reveille and charged accordingly. When he picked up his travel warrant he was given a letter to be handed into the station headquarters of his new unit. We old Locking boys welcomed him back into the fold when he arrived at our new camp after

Boy Entrants

Boy Entrants Band 1947. (This was an Air Ministry publicity photograph but who could tell they couldn't play any of the instruments?)

lunch a few days later. The letter to SHQ was a 'carry forward' of the penalty received from RAF Locking. He must have been one of the few men to arrive at a new station by mid-afternoon, and be on the six o'clock janker parade the same day. A lesser man might have felt demoralised - but he was big enough to shrug off this miscarriage of justice.

There were those who seemed always to be on jankers, and seemingly were unaffected by their loss of freedom and extra duties. There was often discussion and conjecture about who held the record, but it was difficult to equate the claims of some contenders, when they had awarded themselves two 'good conduct' stripes. I never did find out who authorised the award of these stripes.

I'm not sure if it was ever an organised action, but on one occasion there was a total boycott of the six o'clock jankers parade. Not a single defaulter turned up. The camp cinema was showing 'King Kong', and it was a Thursday of the week in which we got paid. Unilaterally, or collectively, it must have been decided that to see the film was worth the risk of missing the parade, and there was always the possibility that the odd man would not be missed. The house was packed, and the cigarette smoke already beginning to cloud the air, when the projector was turned off and the lights turned on. A sergeant strode onto the stage. 'Those of you who should be on defaulters parade have 15 minutes in which to report to the Piquet Post - the rest of you have 15 seconds in which to put out those cigarettes.'

In due course the second entry of Boy Entrants arrived at Locking. Now there was no stopping us! We had seen it all before; so we religiously and 'helpfully' advised our junior colleagues on what to do and how best to do it; who to make friends with if they wanted their new boots to be 'bulled' for a modest sum; which NCO's would turn a blind eye if they saw you smoking, and offered to hide their cigarettes in a safe place, subject to a percentage commission, until the traditional kit search of new intakes was over; offered to share the food parcels they had brought from home, and reluctantly sold them some bars of 'Sgt Major's' soap - essential for scrubbing the barrack room table, and tins of floor polish for their bed spaces, plus a few laundry labels 'to save them the trouble of going to the stores to buy them.' We were not totally pecuniary in our approach, however, we gave them some used razorblades which they would need to have in order to achieve the required 'white

Over and Out 29

Boy Entrants

handle' on the barrack room 'dry scrubber'. Looking back, it is difficult to believe that we were so crafty, and they so gullible. No doubt they had their own back when the third and fourth entries arrived.

As the numbers of trainees grew, so did our awareness of extra-curricular activities and the benefits they could attract. As a member of the football team, or boxing team, there was additional time off for training and different mealtimes with a much improved choice of quantity and quality menu. Being known as a cross-country running enthusiast enabled one to have a less supervised 'sports afternoon'. Out of sight a couple of fields away from the camp, and you could lay undetected and at peace for up to a couple of hours, before panting your way back past the guardroom on your way to the showers.

Bandsmen had time off for practice and were not subjected to such close scrutiny as the rest of us on the Saturday morning parade. Judging by the numbers of broomsticks which were hurled into the air during off-duty periods, there must have been a suppressed Drum Major's mace in every kitbag. There was the same enthusiasm, but far less expertise, in the noises which emanated from the band practice hut. The hesitant drum taps which suggested stiff left wrists, was only outweighed by the tone deafness of the would be trumpeters.

Even being a Roman Catholic enabled one to obtain a much more substantial breakfast after attending early morning Mass. It was most extraordinary how the number of RCs increased as the term progressed. Those under training as Aircraft Finishers had their own particular benefit. Because they were working in a dope laden atmosphere, they were supplied with a mug of cocoa (made with milk) twice a day. Even those that hated the beverage always partook - after all, it was free. We were learning fast the wiles of life and survival of the fittest.

Some of the more 'outdoor' types in our entry maintained that one of the highlights of our 18 month training was the summer camp. For this, we were taken to Braunton near Barnstaple in north Devon. We were herded into a huge field at the base of some hills and confronted with an equally huge pile of canvas which, we were informed, were six man tents. We were then pitched into a new non-aeronautical world of jargon, which included 'duckboards', 'flysheets', 'centre' and 'cross' poles, 'groundsheets', 'drain gullies', 'guy ropes', 'tie ropes' and many others. Thanks to the experience of those who were former Scouts, we were able to lay out the duckboards, dig the drain trenches, erect the tents and protective flysheets, fill our full length sleeping and pillow palliasses with straw, lay them out on our groundsheets and make up our beds, well before the cooks had time to prepare a hot meal for the, by now, starving multitude. Perhaps due to the sweet-smelling hay - or maybe sheer exhaustion - we slept the sleep of the dead that night.

Apart from long route marches; playing cowboys and indians (fieldcraft) over the local terrain; foreign legionnaires (desert survival) around the dunes of Saunton Sands and a visit to RAF Chivenor, my main recollection is of being taken out to dinner by my Aunt and Uncle who lived near Barnstaple. My Mother had let it be known that I was camped at Braunton and my Uncle Charles, who owned a large taxi company in Barnstaple, turned up with my Aunt in a magnificent car to ask if I could go to dinner with them. With trepidation, I approached the Officer Commanding, saluted and asked if I could introduce my Uncle and Aunt. The OC's immediate and only response to me was 'put your hat on straight laddie - you're not Admiral Beatty.' He spoke with my Uncle and Aunt, and then gave permission for myself and a friend to leave camp for the evening. We were taken into Ilfracombe, where we had a blow-out meal at one of the hotels, after which we were returned to camp, each with one of the old white £5 notes 'to tide us over'. Such largesse enabled us to live the life of Riley for several weeks. Small wonder that much of the other activities of the camp do not come easily to mind.

However, I do recall some feeling of satisfaction and relief when we returned to RAF Locking. Somehow, during our absence, our old hutted camp seemed to have acquired a greater level of home comfort, added friendliness and security, than had been evident previously. For some of those with steady girlfriends - our proximity to Weston-super-Mare added a spice to the rather spartan life of recent days.

On recommencing our training after the summer camp, we began to identify ways in which our technical and academic schooling had direct equivalents with our every day service life. Geometry lessons emphasised the fact that there were 360 degrees out from the centre of the camp, and that it was statistically stupid to select a route which would take one past the Piquet Post or Guardroom. Basic physics - heat, light and sound - made us aware that the heat from two 'plate-to-plate' electric irons plugged into light sockets, was sufficient to make edible, though extremely thin toast, that the water from the ablutions was insufficiently hot to make a drinkable cup of Camp coffee, while the hotter water drained from the radiators tasted absolutely vile; that the absence of light was a decided advantage when breaking bounds after dark; and that when secreted inside one's locked steel locker during wet sports afternoons, maintaining absolute silence was essential, if one was to avoid discovery. (There was a certain Corporal Instructor who made a habit of lightly tapping on the steel door and whispering, 'are you alright mate?' (To respond was fatal.)

Not all the 'equivalents' were so self evident. We experienced some confusion concerning 'pressures and velocities within a venturi or convergent duct', on the basis that two Boy Entrants trying to simultaneously squeeze through the hole in the boundary fence adjacent to the Station Commander's

Engineering Drawing Classes

residence, certainly did not equate with 'an increase in velocity and a reduction in pressure'. Our awareness of the strength effect of 'variations in the specific gravity of liquids' technically concerned with aircraft fuel, was enlightened by our exposure to a local brew of cider - obtainable from a nearby farm - which went under the intriguing name of 'tangle-foot'.

With each week that passed we became more and more aware that our time until final

Technical Training Class 1st Entry Sgt Finley Instructing

Boy Entrants

examinations was growing shorter and shorter. Word circulated that the First Entry of Boy Entrants would soon be leaving, and this led to reports of young ladies being seen in tears, waving off boyfriends returning to RAF Locking on the evening bus from Weston. Were these really the same people who had, on our arrival, been so uneasy in the presence of those whom they believed to be 'ex Borstal boys'? It seemed that the only group who would be glad to see the back of us, were the Second Entry. Once we had departed, they would be 'Top Dogs' - so heaven help the next intake!

I don't think any of us regarded our final technical and school exams as anything problematical or unique. We had become so accustomed to periodic testing that the finals were looked upon as just another series of tests. The vast majority passed and obtained their expected grades, and just a few failed. It seemed rather an anti-climax.

Our Passing Out parade was held on 12 November 1948, in conditions which could only be described as inclement.

Just enough drizzle to take the shine off badges, buttons and boots, and to dampen out the knife-like creases we had so painstakingly pressed into our best blues. Nevertheless, we felt both proud and smart, and were complimented as being so by those whose opinions really mattered. The ceremony was attended by parents and friends, and for the last time at RAF Locking, we marched across and around the barrack square; first in column of route and then in review order behind our (now) competent Band. We would have felt deprived if they hadn't played 'Georgia'! Following the taking of the salute by the Air Officer Commanding, we were marched off, back to No 1 Wing, and dismissed. Not as Boy Entrants - but as Airmen.

It had been almost exactly 18 months to the day since we first entered through the gates of RAF Locking. With the hind-sight of half a Century one must admit that those months had made a significant difference to us all. We had arrived as 'recent school leavers' and would depart as trained RAF mechanics. In the words of one instructor, we were 'being turned loose, crammed full of knowledge and totally lacking in experience'. I don't know what he meant by experience, since this expression is capable of many interpretations; but on my own assessment, we had gained experiences over the 18 months which would have taken our civilian counterparts several years to acquire. We had been given the foundations upon which to build a career either within the RAF, or in civil aviation. We had learned the value of companionship, and earned the respect of our compatriots. We had formed friendships with the civil population, which had led to us being accepted by, and establishing bonds with the people of Weston-super-Mare. We had experienced the value of achieving maturity. 'Totally lacking in experience'? Rubbish - we had experienced the values of life and living, and were preparing to apply the practical implications of our theoretical learning. What else could the man expect of an average 17 year old airman?

A few days later we departed from Weston-super-Mare railway station. Waving us off were a number of ladies, some young - many wearing Boy Entrant 'wheels' around their necks; and some older, bidding farewell to their surrogate sons. It was the end of an era, but some would return to renew old friendships.

No 1 Entry Passing Out Parade

Boy Entrants

Mr JW Murphy is curator of the 'BRATS 192' Association. Needless to say, he says, the RAF today is much different from late 1940s.

'Food and clothing were still rationed so everyone had a meal ticket that was marked off in little squares with breakfast, dinner and tea on them. These squares were pierced with a prong of a fork as you got to the hot plate, to stop anyone going around twice. At breakfast and tea you received two slices of bread and a piece of butter or marge about I" square and 3/8" thick. Of course, we were always starving so ate anything in sight. In 1949 about 20 to 30 members of the entry went AWOL as a protest over food. They were away for seven or eight days before being captured or returning voluntarily. The most noteworthy point is that no charges were preferred, although some fatigues were doled out, and the catering officer was moved.

The camp barber used to visit the classrooms where the instructor would decide who needed a haircut whereupon the selected unfortunates would be publicly 'butchered' there and then - at a cost of sixpence.

At Easter 1949 the third entry lads painted one of the sergeant instructor's billet window black so that he would not realise the time and get them up too early, as was his wont.

However, the prank backfired as the whole Wing was paraded on the square and advised that no one would be allowed to go on grant until the culprits owned up. To save great suffering the guilty ones owned up and had to clean off the paint before proceeding on leave.

The following are extracts from Standing Orders Boy Entrants Royal Air Force Station Locking issued by the Officer Commanding No

John Murphy at the NAAFI Wagon

The 3rd Entry Electrical

1st Entry Instrument Mechanics

5 SofTT - August 1949:

• Nothing indicates the smartness of the RAF more than the appearance of Boy Entrants when walking out or marching in the streets, and the manner in which they salute officers. When walking out Boy Entrants are to hold themselves smartly and are not to lounge about in the streets or at street corners.

• Boy Entrants are not to wear, or have in their possession, any article of plain clothes, except flannel trousers for sports purposes.

• Boy Entrants permitted to attend Fancy Dress dances are to be correctly dressed in 'Walking Out Dress' when proceeding to and from the dance. Permission to attend is to be in writing.

• Boy Entrants are not to sing or act in a noisy manner when riding in transport of any description.

• Boy Entrants may proceed outside the Station, in 'Walking Out Dress', to a radius of

Boy Entrants

10 miles without a pass, but must return to camp by 2115 hrs - 2230 hrs depending on rank and good conduct badges. Boy Entrants wishing to proceed beyond the 10 mile radius are to obtain permission from their OC Wing in writing.

• Boy Entrants are to conduct themselves in an orderly manner at all times when in the company of females and are not to walk arm in arm.

• Boy Entrants are to pay scrupulous attention to their personnel cleanliness and health. No self respecting Boy Entrant will allow himself to be dirty and no Boy Entrant can be healthy if he is dirty. A dirty Boy Entrant is offensive to his comrades and a nuisance to all with whom he comes in contact. A bath is to be taken at least twice per week.

Brian Dobbins, writing in BRATS Newsletter, expresses his feelings on being a Boy Entrant.

'All who joined the Boy Entrants had lived through World War Two and with the cessation of hostilities it seemed a good idea to join as Bader, Cheshire, Bennett and company, it all seemed the natural thing to do when we filled in the application form in those well placed advertisements. Arriving at RAF Locking I soon felt that while it was still the Royal Air Force it wasn't the real Air Force, and 18 months seemed a long time away to the day when we would finish training and become men instead of mere boys.

Of course, what RAF Locking did for us was to 'knock us into shape.' It took me longer than most and, in the long term, it was the years after RAF Locking that made a man of me. Love it or hate it our days in the 'Brats' can be looked back on with some nostalgia. The scrumping forays after dark in the orchards close by the camp on a hot summer night, and nearly getting caught when one of us crashed out of a tree.

Who will ever forget that first passing out parade? It wasn't the spit and the polish, it was the bold statement that the 1st Entry had reached maturity and were all leaving, fully trained to take their places among the men. The rest of us would surely follow but in the meantime…

The teenage years are the most difficult of the 'Growing Up' era, and some of us may have felt that we had, in becoming 'Brats', jumped out of the frying pan into the fire, that is exactly how I felt at the time. Many of us asked ourselves, 'What have we done? What are we doing here?' Fifty years on the 1st Entry may well have the answers. My own feelings are that they were good days, and what a pity the youth of today can't have the same opportunity.'

Colin Secker, who still lives in Weston was a Boy Entrant in 1947/48 and recalls the 2nd and 3rd Entries.

'In 1948 the 2nd and 3rd Entries of boy entrants walked off camp en mass until something was done about the quality of the food. This was in effect a mutiny and this was hushed up and brushed under the carpet. The food was absolutely awful to the degree that trainees would break into the food stores of the cook house through the sky light in order to steal the bread. The entrepreneurs obviously saw some profit in this and when they had their fill they would sell the rest. The Mess was a wooden hut in the same position as the current Airmens' Mess and the staff took their life in their hands when they opened the doors, people were so hungry that the staff were nearly trampled in the rush to get fed.

The level of discipline in those days would not be tolerated in today's society but we just took it all in our stride. It was generally accepted that the trainees would show respect to their elders (bearing in mind that we were all very young lads). There was no such thing as hooliganism. We would play tricks on people but it was never very serious, not vandalism for the sake of it. The worst thing I ever did was to cut up the Sergeant Cook's bike. He was a bit of a tyrant and nobody really liked him. One Sunday at about four o'clock (early tea), when I had a pass to go down town, me and a mate were on our way to the Mess for tea. I felt a sharp prod in my back and it was the Sergeant Cook who was jabbing me with a meat cleaver. He told us to go in the kitchens and wash the dishes. My mate went and did what he was told but I didn't. I told him I had a pass for town but he wouldn't listen, anyway I refused to go to the kitchens and was promptly marched to the cells where I spent the night. I never did get to go down town. The next day I was up in front of the CO on a charge and got 14 days jankers. The following day we had a big football match in which I was supposed to be playing so I was called back in front of the CO and he admonished the charge. He also said that he had been waiting all day for me to present him with a redress of grievance but in those days we didn't really know what that was or how the system worked. Anyway, I decided to get my own back on this Sergeant Cook so a few of us stole his bike, took it back to our billet and cut it up into eight pieces. We chained the remains together and put it where he had left it. Next day we were watching from a distance to see what his reaction would be and we saw him riding past on his bike, it turned out that we had cut up someone else's bike. The Sergeant was posted elsewhere shortly after that so he was no longer a problem.

I was on jankers once and the favourite fatigue was to go into the cook house kitchens and scrub the tins. In those days they used great big copper vats to prepare the porridge for the following morning. Anyway, this one time we'd had enough so we put all sorts of things in the vats, greasy clogs, carbolic soap and anything else that we could find. In the Mess hall there was a long table where you placed any items of food that you thought was poor standard so that you could complain about it. The day after the cleaning session this table was piled high with bowls of porridge that people had refused to eat.

I was at RAF Locking from May 1947 to October 1948, and then posted to RAF Bassingbourne. I was called in to see the Warrant Officer who said that I would be going on full pay soon (I was still classed as a boy at this stage), I told him that I already was and so they proceeded to take all the extra pay off me in instalments. I should have kept my mouth shut. I had the last laugh though because boys were entitled to extra leave so I

> *'The food was absolutely awful to the degree that the trainees would break into the food stores of the cook house through the skylight in order to steal the bread. The entrepreneurs obviously saw some profit in this and when they had their fill they would sell the rest.'*

Boy Entrants

took the lot all in one go.

In 1947 there was nothing for us to do in civvy street because of all the demob troops who were looking for work so the young boys didn't get a look in. All that was available was errand boy or something similar so I joined up. I wanted to join as an apprentice but I don't think I had the academic qualifications for it because of the disruption to my education during the war years. I first of all went to North Weale for induction and aptitude testing. I was supposed to be an airframe mechanic. That didn't mean very much because when we first arrived at Locking we were lined up and a tractor with a low loader was driven by us and we had tool kits thrown at us. Depending upon what was in the tool kit decided which trade you were going to be in. Mine had some brand new paint brushes in it so I ended up as a painter and finisher. It had its advantages because, as painters, we got extra cocoa at NAAFI break. There was far too much for us so when we went to collect the urn from the cook house we would make a detour on the way back and sell the cocoa to the other trainees.

One of the favourite methods of getting out of workshop practice was to spend lots of time in the toilets where you could slip off for a crafty fag. One instructor overcame this by cutting up a great big telegraph pole and attaching the toilet keys to it so if you wanted to go to

Boy Entrants

the toilet you had to carry this great big pole over your shoulder.

When we arrived at Locking all of our personal belongings (clothes etc.) were parcelled up and sent home. You were not allowed to keep civvy clothes. On the first leave home I remember that we had to take every bit of kit with us, we couldn't leave anything on camp. We only had best blues and overalls, we didn't have battle dress or working dress of any kind. Everything had brass buttons which had to be really highly polished. In fact everything had to be highly polished and scrubbed, if it could be cleaned then we had to clean it.

The people from Weston first of all thought that we were borstal boys and there were many stories going around the local community about us and why we were there and that is where the nick name Brats originally came from. It didn't take long for those stories to get dispelled. Generally we got on very well with the local people, there was the odd fight in the town but nothing serious. I always remember the local bus station was packed full of lads waiting to catch the last bus back to camp. They were hanging off the platform out of windows anything just to get on the bus. During the week we had a nine o'clock curfew and that was lights out! If you didn't make it back by then you were in trouble. Reveille was about 6.30am and once a week we had to have a bath. Once you had your bath you had to sign the bath book to say that you had bathed and this was checked to make sure that everyone was keeping themselves clean. Bed packs every day were the norm. Not full kit, but your bed had to be laid out in the prescribed manner. Anyone who needed to go to the toilet during the night would take a leak out of the billet window instead of going to the toilets proper. The SWO would look for the tell tail brown patches under the windows and the person whose window that was would get into trouble so the trick was to pee out of someone else's window!

We got 10 bob a fortnight in our hand pay and this was just not enough to live on. If you had any money or rations left towards the end of the fortnight you were a king and everyone wanted to know you. You could get people to clean your things or your bed space and generally do all your billet work for you in exchange for a couple of drags of a cigarette or something to eat.

We had a voluntary band that used to go round and perform at all the local events. It was only a trumpet and drum band but it was pretty good. Although it was voluntary, once you volunteered, that was it you were in for good. I learned the trumpet and the drums and how to change the skin of a drum. That was all slimy and horrible but we had a really good time in the band.

Anything that you put in the communal drying rooms was liable to be nicked so you had to keep a close eye on your stuff. The accommodation was centrally heated with hot water pipes that were fed from a central boiler house taken all over camp on overhead runs. Even so it was still bloody freezing during the colder months of the year.

The Station Commander at the time was Gp Capt Geoffery Paish and he was a Great Britain tennis player. He was quite famous in the sporting world.

Because we were the first Boy Entrants, nobody knew what to expect including the instructors. They had no idea what they were going to get to teach and some of them were a bit heavy handed especially the drill instructors. There were a number of occasions when lads would literally cry themselves to sleep because what had been said and done to them during the day. Nobody ever tried to kill themselves or anything like that but it could be very unpleasant. Some of the lads would come up with all sorts of excuses why they could not get back to camp after a leave period or 72 hour pass, forgot my books, train was delayed, floods (in the middle of summer). One particular lad always turned a 72 hour pass into a week, every time. All character building stuff I suppose. The friends we made became friends for life and lots of us keep in touch even to this day.'

Brian Adam has also reminisced about life as a Boy Entrant in BRATS 192 and reprinted here is the part of his article, 'To Follow a Different Drum' that pertains to life at RAF Locking:

'My father served in the RAF (wartime) and my brothers did their National Service - also in the RAF. Being different (a typical teenager),

Boy Entrants

On Parade for the AOC in 1948

I wanted to go to sea but I was too young - so I joined the Air Force. For one who had been steeped in the lore of the service from giggles to Sgt Braddock VC, (of the Rover and the Hotspur), I was woefully ignorant of the working Air Force. Consequently, at the recruiting office I picked out the most attractive poster and said, 'I want to be like him!' 'Him' in this case happened to be a Boy Entrant!! (I can hear gasps of outrage from the Blimps - but please lads, I did end up as a Brat like you).

I had no knowledge at that time of the hierarchy of the system with Apprentices at the top followed by the 'Boggies' - National Servicemen to the lowest of the low, the Boy Entrant. At least that's how the Leading Apprentice described it when we first met! Nevertheless, I am grateful for my time as a 'Boy', it was all part of life's rich tapestry (I thought I would throw that bit in to show the classical education I received later at Cranwell). In an attempt to broaden the mind of the afore mentioned Leading Apprentice, I would like to tell you how the lower echelons existed.

As 'Boys' we were kitted out at RAF Locking, taught our left foot from our right, how to march in threes and eventually, in some cases literally, pass out. One bitterly cold day the square at RAF Locking was filled with Boys and boggie trainees waiting for the Inspecting Officer, who was probably fortifying himself with sherry in the Mess. Gradually bodies started to appear, Waterloo must have been a doddle compared to this! Unconscious, frost bitten hypothermic men lay on the ground (at attention, of course) and were half carried or dragged to the grassy bank at the edge of the square where a fleet of ambulances ferried them to SSQ, (where they could no doubt be shocked back to consciousness with a cold shower).

Gradually the numbers on the square decreased as the clever ones, after having their bodies deposited on the grass verge, sneaked off between the huts to the security of the NAAFI. My fondest memory of the day was the SWO with his pace stick yelling at the top of his voice 'stop this rot', while the sergeants closed the ranks up for inspection.

Eventually the Reviewing Officer did arrive and was greeted by 'We few, we happy few' (Henry the VIII part six, or was it Henry VI part eight). I like to think that it was the rosy glow of compassion that made him instruct the Parade Commander to do only one march past, but perhaps the hail that was blowing across the parade square from the sea had something to do with it. They were hard men in those days! Brian was later posted to RAF Yatesbury for Radio Mechanic training.

However, a contribution from George Highmore to the BRATS 192 Newsletter is entitled:

Henry was a 'Brat 192'

(by Henry Gee)

'Henry is not good at reunions, because he can't remember names or readily recognise faces that should be familiar. He often attributes a name to the wrong face, but in his extreme maturity he doesn't care as much as he used to. In spite of this tendency to confusion, or perhaps somehow because of it, he is not

Boy Entrants

looking forward to the reunion at the end of the year. He expects to be 'not good at it' and anticipates some perverse pleasure in consequence. At the reunion will be some senior citizens who first met at RAF Locking on 14 October 1947 as the 2nd (Post War) Entry Royal Air Force Boy Entrants. They all had service numbers starting with 192, hence the 'Brats 192' Association which embraces the first few entries.

Discipline

The RAF of 1947 was very different from that of today. The training environment was more like the 'Approved School' of the time, compared to the seats of learning excellence of the 1990s. It was harsh and primitive, with a traditional military discipline rigidly applied. There was 'plenty of stick' and 'little carrot' for Boy Entrants in the daily routine at RAF Locking in 1947.

The period was so close to the end of World War Two that Henry's friends at home thought his choice of career quite daft, and they had joked as he left them that it was bit late to be 'joining up'. Hindsight reveals that the recruits of that period were the 'new blood' of the Royal Air Force, a small replacement for those thousands of weary war veterans then being demobilised. Henry and his mates served for 18 months as trainee aircraft mechanics, during which they experienced the confines of a closed and tightly controlled society, and one in which they were moulded into disciplined military aircraft technicians. A detailed account of that period would quickly bore the reader, but a few anecdotes might draw an interesting contrast between then and now.

Few of those young men were familiar with group discipline and life seemed to become harder as they were introduced to its constraints. They were told with a caustic wit by the first RAF NCO to address them within minutes after arrival that the only activity they would be allowed to indulge in without 'orders' would be to breathe. This, they would be expected to do at all times, without extraneous sound or disturbance to others. They could breathe all day, and all night, indeed to stop breathing without permission would also constitute an offence to good order and discipline.

They would be allowed, indeed required by orders, to sleep between rigidly defined 'off duty' hours. They would be constrained to speak only when spoken to, or ordered to speak. Social talking, or casual discussion, would be allowed during break periods and during 'off duty' hours, but it was to be done quietly.

In moving from place to place they were to march or walk smartly, never in large groups and, while walking 'in one's own time' salute anything in uniform that looked like it might be an officer.

Smoking was forbidden for those under 17 years of age, and only permitted for older 'boys' when granted a 'smoking pass'. Girlfriends were forbidden at any age, except with the express permission of both sets of parents.

In consequence, and in common with all the confined and suppressed of this world, Henry and his comrades did not entirely conform.

Given the slightest opportunity they 'kipped'. They slept or dozed at lectures, or flat on their backs at each break and on Wednesday afternoons, which was designated a 'Sports Afternoon', they crept like rats in a sewer to the nearest concealed corner and slept to great content. It was not unknown on such occasions for the most determined to conceal themselves inside their own or other's wardrobes to enjoy the Wednesday 'kip'. The authorities, always alive to such slothful habits, mounted regular patrols throughout the 'Sports Afternoon', headed by the Station Warrant Officer or the Drill Corporals - they were too often successful. Snoring was of course a dead giveaway, particularly in the confines of a small wooden wardrobe in an otherwise deserted barrack room.

They shouted and argued, harangued and roared at every opportunity. They sang loud and filthy songs after 'lights out' and convulsed

> *'Few of those young men were familiar with group discipline and life seemed to become harder as they were introduced to its constraints. They were told with a caustic wit by the first RAF NCO to address them within minutes after arrival that the only activity they would be allowed to indulge in without "orders" would be to breathe.'*

38 Over and Out

Boy Entrants

when someone with impeccable timing introduced a flatulent percussion. They fought at the slightest pretext.

A few of the more romantic minded sought exceptional permission to court. The only possible route from the barrack room to the arms of a female was via dancing classes allowed under a spartan recreation regime. The aspiring lover would first enrol in dancing classes which were held, under supervision by the Salvation Army, at the local School of Dance in Weston-super-Mare. Processing an application for enrolment took a few weeks during which time the RAF would seek written permission from the applicant's parents. Permission obtained, the applicant made an appointment with the 'Sally Ann' who escorted him and other dancers to the venue where they soon 'clicked' with a girl - it was generally thought that the uniform helped. The liaison was technically an offence until such time that the authorities received the permission of the girl's parents for the pair to go out together. In practice, the boy had first to court the parents before turning legitimate attention to the girl.

There was no TV, video or radio - there were no portable radios. The only concession to entertainment was from the tannoy which relayed the BBC Home Service which one could only hear by pressing an ear to the loudspeaker mounted on the ceiling. It was eventually discovered why the tannoy was so weak when, bringing earphones home from summer leave with the intention of wiring into the system, someone discovered that dozens of others in other barrack rooms had the same idea, only months earlier! This practice was soon discovered by the authorities and outlawed with the inevitable result that the listeners who were caught and punished were those who had only recently discovered the scam.

Boy Entrants wore peaked caps on most parades where they prided themselves in their marching and drill precision, so they slashed and depressed the peaks to resemble guardsmen. Like most rebellious fads, the habit was noticed and, on one particular parade, a spiteful inspecting Officer decided to test the security of those severely slashed peaks by tugging at each in turn. Most came away in his hand leaving that erstwhile impeccable squad of Boy Entrants looking like a bunch of Russian sailors.

Henry and his mates worked hard to become aircraft mechanics and some of them relieved the pressures by pursuing hobbies or reading something trashy like a Hank Janson novel. In sometimes frantic or reckless diversions, they explored the occult via the Ouija board, or made comrades rigid between two trestles to study hypnotism. Some kicked against the constant presence of authority and broke bounds. Having 'broken out' and taken a pint in Banwell village it was necessary to 'break in' again, thus committing a double offence, which if caught at either end meant a period of punishment as a defaulter on 'jankers'. There was no stigma attached to 'jankers'.

On dismissal after a march back from Station workshops they stampeded. They ran, not out of youthful exuberance, but to reach their own

> *'Boy Entrants wore peaked caps on most parades where they prided themselves in their marching and drill precision, so they slashed and depressed the peaks to resemble guardsmen. Like most rebellious fads, the habit was noticed and, on one particular parade, a spiteful Inspecting Officer decided to test the security of those severely slashed peaks by tugging at each in turn. Most came away in his hand leaving that erstwhile impeccable squad of Boy Entrants looking like a bunch of Russian sailors.'*

bedspace as soon as possible to ensure that no 'off duty skiver' had stolen knife, fork, spoon, mug or peaked cap which regulations directed should be displayed upon folded bedding. Roaring into the barrack room, Henry was one best able to take in at a glance any omissions from the displayed kit and, without stopping, accelerate into another room and swipe an identical replacement form the nearest undefended bed. There was no perceived shame in this since the authorities deemed it an offence to lose such items.

At weekends the discipline dissipated completely. The gathering and hungry mob outside the locked and barred dining room doors would push and shove and heave against creaking woodwork well before

Boy Entrants

scheduled meal times. A great cobra head of heaving bodies tried to force those at the front through the dining room doors to the uninspiring, luke warm fare, that had been prepared hours previously. The regular RAF catering staff devised ways to release the bolts on those doors while keeping clear of the flood of humanity that would inevitably burst through.

Henry and his friends smoked and bartered cigarettes, dependent on their relative wealth, age and ability to acquire the forbidden weed. Only a very few were over 17 years old and in possession of a 'smoking chit'. For the majority it was an illegal act and worthy of great cunning. For those over 17, it was a source of great relative wealth. At that time cigarettes cost between 1s 6d - 2s for a packet of 20. Boy Entrants were paid 14 shillings every two weeks. On the face of it, all were equally poor but the black market in cigarettes, evolved by the most enterprising, was a way out of the poverty trap. Many became 'baccy barons'. The exchange rate and barter value was astonishing. A single whole cigarette retailed for about a penny but could be exchanged for up to sixpence. The nearer to the fortnightly

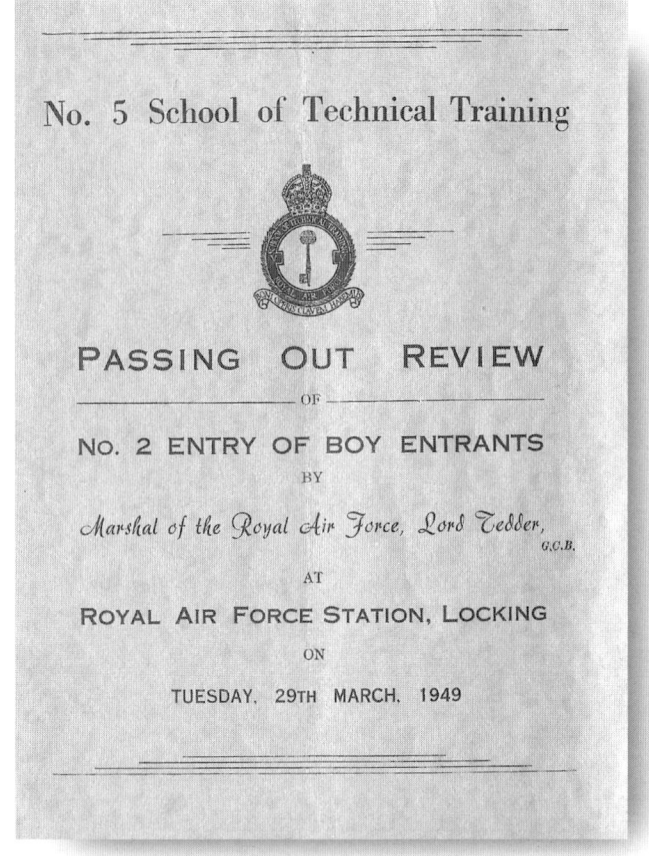

No. 5 School of Technical Training

PASSING OUT REVIEW

OF

NO. 2 ENTRY OF BOY ENTRANTS

BY

Marshal of the Royal Air Force, Lord Tedder, G.C.B.

AT

ROYAL AIR FORCE STATION, LOCKING

ON

TUESDAY, 29TH MARCH, 1949

Passing Out Review No 2 Entry

pay day, the more active the sales and barter became. A 'part smoked fag' could secure the cleaning of one's bed space for a week. For a 'soggy dog end', Henry could get his boots 'spit and polished' ready for the morning parade.

The 2nd Entry had its share of softies and a few loonies at the extremes, but the great majority always defended the one from the other. The 2nd Entry survived the course, nobody died during it, none deserted and only a few served less than their term.

Finally, what is generally not known was that trainees were marched back and forth to work behind a band. Trevor (Nobby) Marwood was the 1st Entry's Drum Major for the formed 'Boy Entrant' Drum and Trumpet band. As new entries arrived the band grew to over 50 trumpets and 20 drums and paraded every day leading the troops to and from classes twice a day and performed for formal parades on and off the Station.'

As a postscript, in May 1997 some 37 ex Boy Entrants attended the 50th Anniversary Reunion at the Bay Side Hotel in Weston. At that dinner a plaque commemorating the event and acknowledging the close ties with the town was presented to the Mayor.

FIRST ENTRY BOY ENTRANTS R.A.F. LOCKING ~ 1947

This plaque commemorates the Fiftieth Anniversary Reunion of the First Post-war Entry of Boy Entrants trained at R.A.F. Locking in 1947

Weston-super-Mare - May 1997

The 50th Anniversary Plaque

The parable of the Erkites

(Reproduced in part from an Airwaves Article published in 'Willy's Corner' submitted by Flt Lt 'Willy' Williams (Ret'd).

And it came to pass in the land of the RAF, in the province of Somerset at a place that is called Locking, there dwelt many strange tribes - the Erkites, the NCOites and the Officerites. Even those of the tribe WAAFites did well among them. And they did toil together, the one with the other, to what end no man knoweth. And at the gate of this place was a sign bearing the inscription, 'Beware of the Bull'.

And it was the custom, at the rising of the sun for the tannoy to speak unto the tribes, saying, 'Wakey, Wakey. Arise all ye who slumber for it is yet day.' And at this command would the tribes arise with much moaning from their slumbers and put on their raiments and go forth to partake of strong and curious foods in their eating places. Thereafter would they depart each unto his appointed place of toil, where they were bound rigid until the setting of the sun.

And there was one among them, an erkite, who, being tired and weary, did not rise with his comrades, but slept soundly after they had departed. It came to pass that his name came before one of the tribe of NCOites, a mighty man, an overseer who did wear a King's crown upon his sleeve. The overseer arose and did go to the dwelling of the erkite and did awaken him with these words, 'what aileth thee O erkite? What cooketh?' And the erkite answered, 'go away', or some such translation for he was of the Barbary Tribe and spake only in their tongue.

Then was the overseer exceedingly wroth and did lift up his voice and say all manner of things to the erkite, even doubting the accuracy of his birth certificate. And he did say unto him, 'Erkite, thou art truly in the fertiliser, thou hast had thy chips.' But it availed him nought and the overseer's view was exceedingly dim. And he did leave the dwelling place uttering 'verily this erkite doth give me the screaming abdabs.'

Then did the overseer enter into the abode of the High Priest, who wore the King's Coat of Arms on his sleeve, and he did say, 'Master, there is one of the tribe of erkites who yet slumbereth, he is as one dead, and uttereth strange words in the erkite tongue claiming to be fireproof.' And when he heard these things the High Priest arose and was much agrieved saying, 'I say unto you that this man should be placed on a fizzer, for he is a dead loss.' And so it was done for there was much of what is deposited by the ox in the land.

And in the fullness of time was the erkite placed before the chamber of the King to await judgement. And the King's councillors did run backwards and forwards with much slamming of doors and the asking of questions, the answers of which they knew not, for their thumbs were deeply inserted. As the erkite stood before the portal, the King's voice was lifted up unto the tannoy summoning the prophets Adminalot, Technicalot and Noalot into his presence. But these prophets did not appear, for they heard not - or so they said. And the erkite seeing this thought to himself, 'tis is a shaky do for I am about to be shafted.'

After much waiting the erkite was ushered into the presence of the King, the mighty one who did adorn himself with four rings on his raiment and much fruit salad on his headdress. And the erkite with much fear and trembling didst clench his buttocks together so as not to annoy the King further, for he could see the King was wrath and was wearing his headdress. The King had set before him tablets of stone bearing the mystic symbol of the High Priest - F252. And the King raised up his voice and asked whether he was of the tribe of the erkites and that his name was Joe. And the erkite answered, 'Yea, O King, I am Joe of the

The Parable of the Erkites

family soap and I toil in the abode of Sir Technicalot in IT.' Then did the King say, 'Have ye aught to say, O ye of meagre clues. Why hast thou done this thing? Thou knowest that only those of the tribe of Officerites with two and one half and three rings on their raiment are allowed to lie abed, for they are not blessed and anointed.'

And the erkite did reply, 'I knoweth these things, for I have all the gen, but upon the night before, I went into the land of the NAAFI-ites, and thou knowest O King, that they are nought but thieves and robbers, yea, even ration wanglers.

And they didst take from me all my sliver and gave me strange liquor in return and there was much iniquity in this place. Verily I was as the proverbial newt. And lo in the morning at the sunrise I was as lead and could not awaken, neither did I hear when the tannoy spake unto all the tribes.'

And the King, on hearing this tale of cock and bull, smote his altar in his wrath and did tear the erkite off a mighty strip. The erkite spake to the king saying, 'Does this mean that I am about to get the chop for this deed?' And the King answered, 'Thou shouldn'st chuckle, thou laggard, verily thou shalt be punished, thou has had thy last chance, thou hast dropped one. Be off, and remove thy finger.'

The erkite was sent forth in double quick time, with much wailing, to abide in the dungeon, known as the Guardroom. There he was stripped of his possessions which were placed in the King's Benevolent Fund.' And in the dungeon, holding high office, were those of the tribe of NCOites who were not as other men, for they were of the tribe RAF Police, whose brightness did not exceed that of Toc H Lamp.

And they did laugh and jeer at the erkite for they knew he was at their mercy and for his crimes they didst revile him with *mysterious utterances which can be loosely translated to mean, 'tough s......t'.*

RAF Locking's own

Not many people realise that when the last tranche of married quarters were being built the digging uncovered the site of a Roman settlement. The following is a copy of an article written in 1958 on the excavations of the married quarter site:

Domestic Bliss in Married Quarters 250 AD

'The first occupation of the area dated from the pre-Roman Early Iron Age, and consisted of a hut and several ditches. Next, after a period of abandonment, a primitive hut was built (middle of the second century AD).

This lasted until about the year 250 AD when it was deliberately destroyed and replaced by the third stone building. Successive periods of rebuilding of this stone building occurred until occupation finally ceased towards the end of the fourth century. Since then, apart from a possible 17th century barn, the area has remained unoccupied until the construction of the present Airmen's Married Quarters, the building of which disclosed the existence of the site. The excavation of the stone building has presented many problems, as can be seen from the plan.

Difficult

The whole area was rendered exceedingly difficult by the large number of modern trenches, which have of course completely destroyed the Roman levels. There are also several concrete paths under which excavation was generally impossible. Finally the modern roadway and a house have completely covered parts of the building so that the plan obtained must, of necessity, be incomplete in many ways. However, despite this apparently

Roman Villa

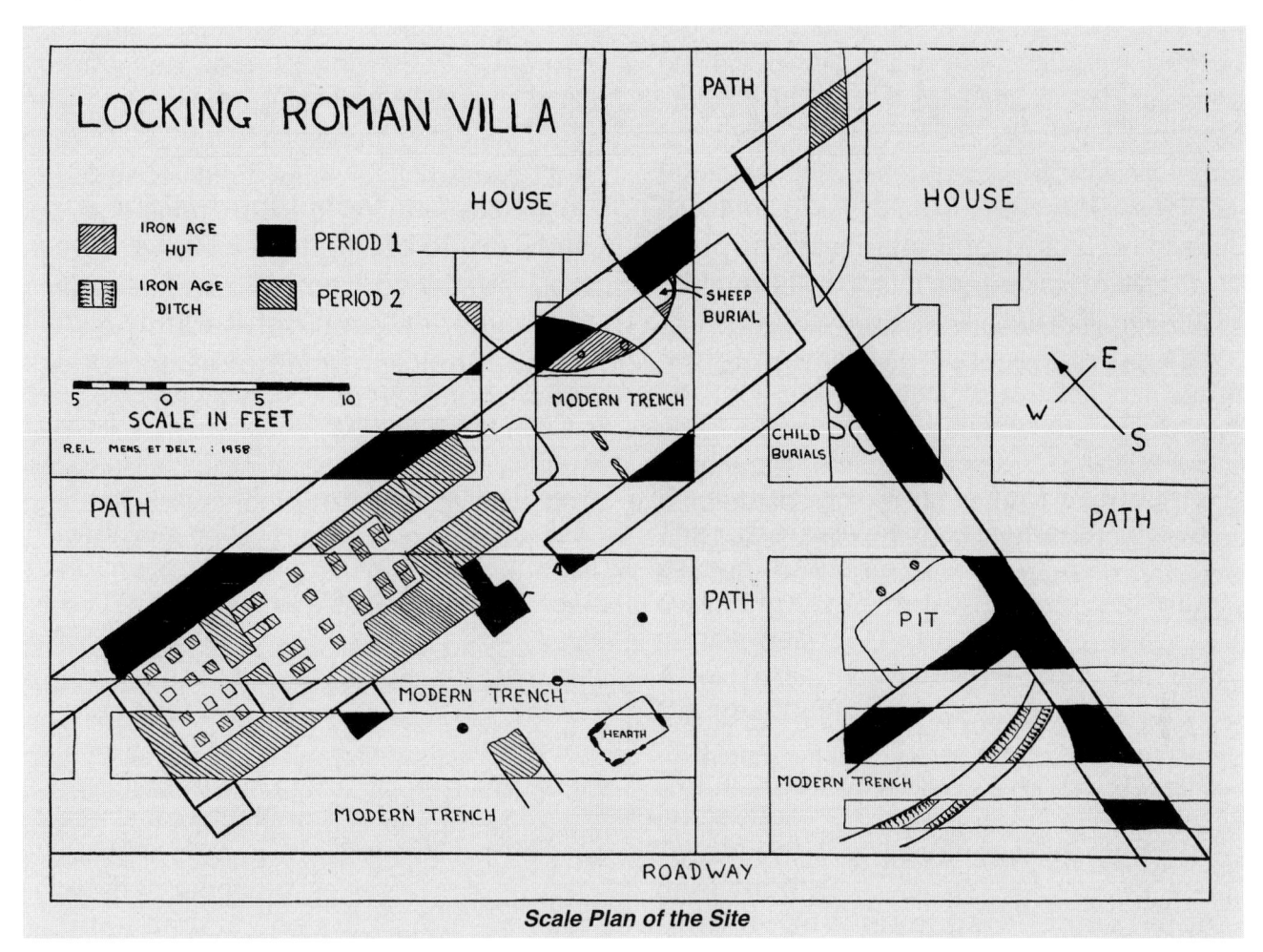

Scale Plan of the Site

hopeless set of circumstances we feel that we have obtained sufficient evidence to give the history of the building Pre-Roman occupation (50BC to 70 AD).

This consisted of a circular Iron Age hut with a clay floor and timber and clay walls supported by posts set round the edge of the hut, two of which can be seen in the plan. The hut was surrounded by a ditch about three feet deep, part of which has been found under the later building.

After the destruction of the hut the area remained derelict until the construction of the stone building. The stone building Period One (mid third century) consisted of a rectangular building approximately 85' by 35', with its long axis running from East to West. It is of a typical Roman type known as 'Basilican' from its superficial resemblance to the aisled Basilica or public hall of Roman towns. It would probably have looked like a large barn with the roof internally supported by a double row of pillars on rammed stone foundations. The walls of the building also had rammed stone foundations, with the whole of the superstructure of wood.

As can be seen from the plan, towards the end of the building the pillar system was replaced by two continuous walls forming internal rooms. Apart from this the internal divisions of the building would all have been of timber, a possible partition screen being shown by the three postholes on the plan. This seems to have been associated with the hearth which was placed in the normal central position, and probably screened the hearth from a doorway directly behind (the postholes for the door are marked on the plan between the last pillar base and the continuous wall).

Child burials

Belonging to this period were the three child burials inserted through the clay floor of the building where shown, two of which had been premature births and the other probably died at birth; it was quite a normal practice to bury

RAF Locking's own Roman Villa

any child that died at birth in such a position.

The most interesting single find of this period was the skeleton of a sheep. It had been buried in a side room during the construction of the building with the head of the animal having been cut off and placed at its feet. Thus it must have been a ritual sacrifice and foundation burial. This is particularly interesting as so far it seems to be the only such example of the sacrifice of a sheep found in Britain.

The stone building, although much superior to the primitive hut, is still a fairly poor type of habitation. For not only would the family live in it, but also the farm animals would be kept and the farm produce stored in other parts of the same building. Despite its simple character it seems to have lasted until the end of the third century when the building was demolished and a superior series of buildings fitted into the ruins.

Radical

In Period Two (circa AD 300), the rebuilding consisted of a radical alteration of the plan with, however, most of the Period One walls being used again as foundations for the new stone built walls. The new plan basically consisted of a bath block inserted in the north 'aisle' of the Period One building and what was probably the living wing of the new house situated at the end of a connecting corridor. This living wing has been almost completely destroyed by a modern house, all that remains being a portion of corridor wall (shown to the northeast of the main building). In order, from east to west, the bath block consisted of a stokehole, furnace flue, hot room with hot bath, and a warm room. A cold plunge bath must also have existed, and at the western end of the bath block an extensive mediaeval pit probably marks its site. The floors of the heated rooms were supported on pilae, that is pillars formed of square tiles, so that the hot air from the furnace could pass under the floor and then up through hollow flue tiles in the walls, thus giving quite efficient central heating. Large quantities of painted wall plaster were obtained from the filling of the heated rooms, the decoration consisting of lines and dots in yellow and green on a white background. The roof of the bath block was of sandstone slabs fixed by iron nails. Finally in the filling of the furnace flue was found the remains of a roof tinial of carved stone, this was the Roman equivalent of a chimney pot.

The rest of the end of the Period One building was rebuilt as one large room with a large pit in one corner. This was probably used as a latrine pit, and was screened by a wooden partition, two postholes of which were found as shown. The rest of this room probably acted as a fuel store and possible servant quarters.

'Squatter'

Period Three (circa 350- 370 AD) represents a large scale rebuilding of the villa, probably due to worsening economic conditions. The bath block was dismantled and levelled, and the adjoining room was refloored with broken roofing slabs and flue tiles. In the last phase of the occupation the building was used for an increasingly untidy 'squatter' occupation which lasted at least as late as the end of the fourth century, until the building probably became too unsafe to live in. No signs of a violent end to the occupation were found. With this the site was abandoned until some time in the mediaeval period when stone robbers from neighbouring villages removed most of the better stone from the walls, luckily, however, missing the brick pilae of the bath block. The finds from the site have been numerous, an especially interesting group of pottery being found in the stokehole and furnace, although on the whole rather poor in quality. Several of the finds are now on show in Weston-super-Mare Museum, and all the finds will finally be presented to the Museum.'

> 'The most interesting find of this period (Period One - mid third century) was the skeleton of a sheep. It had been buried in a side room during the construction of the building with the head of the animal having been cut off and placed at its feet. Thus it must have been a ritual sacrifice and foundation burial. This is particularly interesting as so far it seems to be the only such example of the sacrifice of a sheep found in Britain.'

Training Times

Adult Training and the National Service

In the 1950s and early 60s, in addition to Apprentice Training, RAF Locking was home to adult trainees who were trained as mechanics or fitters on a variety of courses:
- Ground Wireless Mechanics
- Wireless Fitter (Long Course)
- Ground Wireless Fitter (Advanced Training Part 2 Spec)

They were trained in No 3 Wing, which was heterogeneous made up of National Servicemen, short term regulars, long term recruits and airmen remustering to a mechanics trade. There was a sizeable population, for example in 1958 1,803 mechanics and 861 fitters passed their courses.

Alex Dow was conscripted as a National Serviceman in October 1957 after serving an apprenticeship with Ferranti. After recruit training at RAF Cardington and RAF Bridgenorth he arrived at RAF Locking for specialist training, where he was subsequently upgraded and spent a further four years as an equipment instructor before leaving the Royal Air Force. He takes up the story:

'We had one weeks leave, then proceeded individually to our respective training stations, RAF Locking in my case, already known to me from my first ATC Summer Camp. Throughout square-bashing, I had not participated in any of the Trade Aptitude Tests because of my Ferranti Apprenticeship and Heriot Watt studies, always being told to disappear as I

A Regular WAAF Junior Technician in the late 50s/early 60s working on Radar Office Equipment

Trainees in 3 Wing 1954

was already listed for RAF Locking as an Instructor. At RAF Locking, it turned out that about five of us in that entry had been told somewhat similar stories and were therefore very surprised to kind ourselves in a class starting off with Basic Electricity. We protested about this, pointing out that it was a complete waste of both our time and the RAF's for us to cover subjects with which we were extremely well acquainted. (An ex-UAS recruit, Gerrie, reckoned that the 10 weeks total RAF Basic Electricity, Magnetism and Radio courses covered what had taken him two years at University!) Our appeals, phrased in official, very begging supplicant terms, went up the chain of command quite rapidly. In one day, they were turned down by the Gp Capt OC. Fortunately, the Section Leader Instructor reckoned that I had a very strong case and recommended that I try again. This time my appeal reached the Air Vice Marshal at Training Command Headquarters and was granted, subject to me taking a Trade Test. Passing this also brought about immediate promotion to Senior

Over and Out 45

Training Times

Aircraftman.

As a result, I leapfrogged over all of the basic courses to the final part of an equipment course, to familiarise myself with GCA Radar, VHF Radio, Diesels, Hydraulics and Refrigeration. I then took an Instructional Techniques Course which was extremely good and intensive and then I started as an Instructor in about August 1958.

About six members of the course I jumped into were going to dancing classes in Weston-super-Mare. This stimulated me to eventually achieving Silver Medal status, I also did about 90 per cent of the Gold Medal work. It led to my getting to know many Weston people and meeting the Welsh Nurse, Margaret Thomas, who is my wife of many happy years.

The cheque's in the post

About two months after my successful appeal and promotion, I was as usual on Pay Parade in No 3 Block Hall. Four Parades took place simultaneously around the sides of the hall, with the sort of background noises expected from about 400 men present, as well as the usual, much louder parade commands and responses. Each parade faced two tables, at which were sat an officer, sergeant and airman, the latter two from Pay Accounts. The officer could be from any section on the station. The airman had the Pay Records for everyone on that parade. He read out the name. The recipient would reply with his number, the airman then would then read out the amount. Finally, the sergeant would count the cash, pass it to the officer who would count it again, by which time the recipient would have marched up to the table and saluted. The money was handed over, the recipient marched away and the procedure was then repeated etc. The typical pay was about 30 shillings (£1.50) for NS men; and Two Pounds 10 shillings (£2.50) for Regulars. Civilian wages were about £10 to £12 per week, a Regular Corporal about £7.

On this particular Thursday after some others had been paid the following catechism took place:

The Airman - 'DOW'
Me - '857, Sir'
The Airman - 'Thirty-Eight Pounds Fifteen Shillings' (£38.75)
The Officer - 'Pardon?'
The Airman - '38 Pounds, 15 Shillings'
The Officer - 'Are you sure?'
The Airman -'Yes Sir, here it is Sir'
By now, the other Pay Parades have halted, there is silence.
The Sergeant checks my Pay Record.
The Sergeant - 'That's what is down here, Sir. It looks correct'
By now I have marched out and saluted.
The Officer - 'Let me see that'
The Sergeant explains the details to the Officer.
The money is counted by the Sergeant, then the Officer.
The Officer turns to me - 'Count that carefully'
Me - 'Yes, Sir', (taking off my beret and scooping the cash into it.)

In fairness to the Officer, Pay Accounts were only allowed to draw £5 more cash than the Pay Parades required, so for a Station of about 3,000 men, £5 contingency was not much in around £15,000. Also his wages would be about £12 per week before messing etc was taken out, so if the error was deemed to be his, he would have difficulty in re-imbursing the RAF.

Uniform matters

Easter that year, I had a week's leave at home. Our neighbour's son, George Lothian, was also in the RAF, having started as an apprentice and had reached sergeant by then. His mother had been a needlewoman or seamstress, so had sewn on many of her son's badges as he was promoted. On seeing mine, she asked how they had been done as they appeared to be embroidered directly on the uniform material. They were in fact, non-standard but issue badges on grey-blue cloth, which I had very carefully trimmed, then sewn on in such a way that the thread was almost invisible. Surprisingly, the standard badges were the paint-stencilled ones on plain black cloth, far from attractive. I replaced the brass buttons, buckles and badges with 'Stabrite' anodised aluminium ones, avoiding cleaning. Apart from being a slightly different tint from the official brass ones, the Crowns on the Stabrites were the Queen's or St. Edward's Crown; while the brass crowns were still the King's or Imperial Crown dating from the reign of King George VI, who had died in 1952. It was about 1960 before the 'new' Crown appeared on the official issue.

```
R.A.F.                    THE                        R.A.F.
Uniform Badges                                       Collars,
Buttons and      Men's Wear Shop                 Ties, Cravats
Accessories                                       and Scarves
              46 REGENT STREET, WESTON-SUPER-MARE
                       Telephone 146
                  APPROVED STOCKISTS
   of Apprentice Walking-out Dress and Ex-Apprentice Society Ties and Squares
              also Blazer Badge Specialists in
              Gold & Silver Wire or Silk Woven Badges
       Quotation Free    Any Design Made to Order    Quick Delivery
    We cordially invite you to call and inspect without obligation our large stock of
   BLAZERS  SPORTS JACKETS  RAINCOATS  SUITS  TROUSERS  PULLOVERS  GLOVES  TIES & SOCKS  SHIRTS, Etc.
```

Promotion at last

In the July, I had finished the familiarisation course, passing out in the conventional manner as a Junior Technician; and was informed that I was now a Corporal, although neither were promulgated to my knowledge. I took charge of a billet in the middle of the front row of No 3 Wing, Hut 154' which was to be my home for the rest of my time in the RAF.

(I had been in Hut 164 for the 1949 ATC Summer Camp, Hut 142 for the three days of the basic electricity period, Hut 105 for the four months familiarisation. As well as Hut 154, I eventually took charge of 153, 155 and 156. The whole wing, except for one isolated hut beyond the Mess, was demolished by 1986, leaving a wide expanse of grass and about two yards of the path which had split No 3 Wing in two between Huts 152 and 154.)

Being late summer, shirt sleeves was the general order of the day. Frequently, NCO stripes were not visible, as the mounting band would slip down into the rolled-up sleeves.

View of the Hutted Camp looking towards the Water Tower

Training Times

There was consternation among the mainly regular occupants of the hut about two weeks later, when due to rain, I wore my working blue blouse complete with SAC's three-bladed Propeller. At the Squadron Office, the Chief just about had a heart attack when he saw the Props. I pointed out that my promotion had not been promulgated, he immediately asked for my Form 1250, Identity Card, wrote in the 'promotion' and made out a chit for stripes or chevrons. So was I now a Corporal officially? First things first, I was being paid as a Corporal!

Me, an instructor?

In September 1958, I went to RAF Spitalgate near Grantham for the Instructional Techniques Course. Lasting three weeks, it is the most intensive and satisfying course I have ever been on. We frequently were working from 6am to 2am the following morning. Returning to RAF Locking, I embarked upon my teaching career. This taught me a lot, both about the equipment involved and how to present the information to suit the trainees in the classes, who could range from 'intelligent van boys' to PhDs in Physics and the like; and from the two year National Service men to Regulars. The mix of trainees was extremely beneficial, the Regulars generally having been on operational stations as mechanics; and the fact that they were living in something like boarding school conditions.

One sleepy afternoon, I was covering the dangers of some of the equipment such as radio-active valves, not a very inspiring subject. The fluorescent tubes of that era were more dangerous than today's because of the barium and caesium compounds used. One trainee, Harry, from Liverpool asked if he could mention his experience. He was an electrician and had been working with a colleague on scaffolding, changing tubes. His partner had dropped one, cutting himself on the broken glass. He reassured Harry that he was all right. Harry turned back to his work. About 30 seconds later, he sensed that something was wrong and turned to find his workmate bright red in the

Training Times

face and having difficulty breathing. Ten minutes later, the lad was dead. At last, the class sat up, realising that here was a good reason for listening to the lesson.

The main equipment I taught was GCA, Ground Controlled Approach Radar, mounted in large trailer vehicles. The S- band equipment working at 3,000MHz and was used for 360 degree search purposes with a range of about 30 miles. The X-band radar was focused into a small cross using two aerials, elevation and azimuth, scanning alternately in both planes, I did manage to get it working to 30 miles. The X- band aerial structures were special waveguide, with about 110 dipoles spread along them. One wall of the waveguide could move in and out, changing the wavelength in the guide, hence changing the phase of the feeds to each dipole. The resultant wave front from the group of dipoles swung to and fro, creating the scanning effect. The trailers would be parked about 50 yards to the left of the runway as viewed by the approaching pilot, near the remote end, and were also turned about two degrees towards the runway to ensure coverage of the touch-down point in azimuth. Below the trailers were four oleo legs similar to an aircraft undercarriage. These were used to get the two-degree vertical tilt. As the trailers were American designed for use in all climates, they included about 10KW of electric heaters and also refrigeration plant.

Associated with the trailers were 'prime movers' or large trucks, Whites, MACKs or Antars; which also carried 120KW Diesel-electric generating sets. These diesels were started by handcranking, requiring at least two men, preferably three. There were in fact two each of the main transmitting and receiving units in the radar systems, one working, one on stand-by. To communicate there were six VHF RT sets.

Being American, the original switches were 'Up' for 'On' while later British modification or replacement ones were 'Down' for 'On'. With about 200 switches all told, scattered around the truck, some on a big switch panel, others hidden, the trainees could have a 'shocking' time trying to make the equipment safe to work on. There was very little human space in the trailers, a narrow corridor running almost its length, about four feet wide with four seats for the controllers plus two or three maintenance types. It was rather like being in a midget submarine control area. As diesels ignite through compression, it was essential to get them turning over very quickly by hand before kicking in the decompression bar. Classes would struggle over this until the lesson sunk in. Some of the prime movers were 'Diamond T' vehicles, still seen today in use for motorway recovery and heavy haulage. Another unusual item that I looked after at times was a ship-type diesel engine with one foot (300mm) diameter pistons, used to generate 110V, 60Hz supplies for the various American equipments in No 2 Block. Its starter motor was a fair sized petrol engine, charging up compressed air cylinders, which were then used to kick the big engine over.

So as Radar Instructors teaching the technical aspects, principles and practice and outlining the operator's functions, we had to cover a wide variety of subjects and equipment, apart from also teaching Admin, Drill and other General Duty requirements.

Motor vehicles - 1

In February 1959, two of the trainees in my hut were involved in a road accident just outside of the camp. One owned a motor-bike and they were using it to go home to London on the Friday evening of a '48 hour' weekend. (There were many accidents involving motorcycles in the 1950s and 60s). Just beyond the camp boundary, a farm road joined the main road. A car driven by an elderly man shot out on to the main road in the bike's path. The two airmen were taken to Weston General Hospital. The first I knew about it was meeting the pillion passenger unexpectedly on the Saturday morning, coming out of the billet, his face bruised and scarred. He told me what had happened. Later that morning, I went to the hospital and found the ward where the other airman was. I walked up to a very small nurse and asked her who was in charge. 'I am' was the reply. She took me to the airman; and he asked me to bring some of his personal items in. He and his class completed their course shortly afterwards. I saw to the repair of his motorbike and its return to his parents as he had been posted to Cyprus.

I had a half-share in a 1934 Vauxhall saloon

car with another instructor. Later I purchased a 1935 Hillman Minx Estate with spare engine and gearbox for £5, which I later sold for £1. (Due to being laid up for most of World War Two and there being only about 2.5 million vehicles on the road, second-hand cars were usually about 15 to 20 years old). We ran them on a mixture of petrol and paraffin, the sumps were filled with used oil from the local garage at Locking which was still running a taxi that I had travelled in during the 1949 ATC Camp, when about 10 of us had squeezed into it. The cars were parked in one of four Bellman hangars on camp which during World War Two had contained aircraft for instructional purposes although Locking itself did not have an airfield. One night another instructor drove his car through the closed doors at one end of the parking hangar, knocking one section off the rails and bending it about twenty feet up. There was hardly a scratch on the car.

On an earlier occasion, I had travelled in the same car back to camp. The instructor was drunk, missed one obvious opening by 400 yards, and bounced from one side to the other of the narrow sunken back road to Locking village. Never again will I knowingly travel with a drunk driver.

Aircraft raid at Locking

Outside the hangars on the tarmac were the major remains of a Mosquito and a Lancaster. I could remember them from the 1949 ATC Camp. The apprentice classes on passing out after three years training, got up to high jinks. One of the Sergeant Instructors was in charge of the night guard, which was made up of a class of airman trainees, two pairs going out on patrol for two hours at a time. About 20 minutes after the 4am changeover, one patrol rushed back into the Guard Hut.

Airmen - *'Sergeant, there is a big aeroplane in the Married Quarters!'*
Sergeant - *'Are you two imagining things?'*
Airmen - *'No, Sergeant, there really is a big plane in the Married Quarters.'*

The Sergeant turned to the relieved patrol and asked them if they had seen anything unusual in that area - they hadn't. So everyone got into the Sergeant's car and he drove slowly through the very thick mist towards the Married Quarters. Sure enough, just at the start of the MQ, there was a big aeroplane, the remains of the Lancaster. The MT section struggled for three hours with tractors and lorries to move it back to the tarmac; but had to give up. The apprentice class responsible got it back in 15 minutes. They had taken about 30 minutes between patrols to move it uphill, avoiding the guy wires of two radio masts, between the four hangars, turned it at right angles towards the MQ and missing a telephone kiosk, a total distance of about 500 yards on very soft tyres.

Shortly afterwards, both aircraft were broken up on site, the Mosquito carcass showing the basic wooden construction of that very unusual, very useful, aircraft.

Foreign times

The summer of 1959 was very hot, I got suntanned and slightly burned for the first time. There were a lot of charges of self-inflicted injuries around that year; and I can remember seeing some trauma and coma cases from it. There was also a water shortage. This weather suited a new group of trainees, a squad of Iranians. Foreign forces sent suitable individuals for training on, to them, new equipment, but this time it was a group of officers and NCO's who were to establish, in part, a temporary Iranian training group, to

Training Times

teach classes of others with a lesser knowledge of English. As a result, I had one class for a quick, two-day course on GCA, consisting of three Irani, two Iraqi, one Indonesian, one Englishman and one Scotsman. I noted at other times: Chileans, Venezuelans and Germans.

The senior Irani officer was Captain Siraudi who had been the captain of the Irani 1956 Olympics Basketball team. During his period at Locking, about two years, he played for the RAF team. He also offered me a teaching commission in the Iranian Air Force. Shortly afterwards, I met the first regular Iranian class. They were lying on the banking of one of the air raid shelters during a break between classes. One pointed to the ice cream van (so much for security) that came on to camp, asking what it was. I explained that it was a 'Wall's Ice Cream Van'. 'What this Wall's?' they wanted to know. 'The owner, the company that it belongs to.' I replied.

'Owner, company?' How could I explain this concept?

'Safi-Yari's Ice Cream!' I explained. Corporal Safi-Yari was the spiv, the fly-merchant among them. They seemed to understand 'Wall's' after that. It certainly caused great hilarity.

It was something I ate

On 1 September, I was in the theatre of the old Weston General Hospital on the Boulevard having my appendix removed.

I had reported sick on the Monday and was given kaolin, the MO thinking it was a simple 'tummy upset'. That night, I vomited violently and did not get to sleep until 4am on the Tuesday. I woke at 6am, feeling great, the sun was shining brightly.

Having cycled to the Mess for breakfast, I was unable to eat anything, so I reported sick once more. The same MO saw me initially, then had me rushed into the Senior Medical Officer in the adjacent surgery, the poor hapless airman in there being unceremoniously bundled out with his trousers around his ankles.

The SMO examined me thoroughly; but did not say what his diagnosis was. Instead, he sat looking at the phone and said, 'Wroughton or Weston' a few times. I realised he was trying to decide whether to have me taken to Weston General Hospital or to RAF Wroughton Hospital. So, I said 'my fiancee is a nurse down in Weston.' 'Right, Weston it is' he said. He phoned and made the necessary arrangements. The RAF ambulance crew came in to stretcher me out, I wanted to walk. 'No, you might fall and injure yourself', they said. I lay down on the stretcher, it was lifted up; but would not pass through the door, I almost fell off as they struggled with the load. I got off the stretcher, we walked through the door, I lay down on the stretcher again and was carried to the ambulance. One of the crew said he would take my bike back to my billet later.

We set off for the hospital, bells ringing. The first part of the journey was reasonable, as the road from just east of the camp to the first railway bridge on the outskirts of the town is fairly straight and wide, having been built at the start of World War Two to allow aircraft built in a Shadow Factory in the valley beyond the camp to be towed, generally by horses, down to Weston airfield by the railway bridge. But the two bridges, main line and town line, were hump backed and skewed relative to the road, so I left the stretcher a few times on that part of the journey. The driver would not let me take over. It also transpired that neither he nor his colleague knew where the hospital was! So I sat up in the back, shouting directions over the din of the bells.

On the following Sunday after the operation, I was moved to a private room attached to a Women's ward. One of the Staff Nurses thought that I should have a change of pyjamas, my RAF ones being covered in yellow aquaflavine. She produced a pair of woman's ones, rose pink and dotted with little bunches of flowers. Later when I was able to get up, I would don my working blue top and trousers over these, walking about the hospital and sitting out on the veranda which overlooked the Boulevard, a major shopping street in Weston. After two weeks in the hospital, I was transferred to the Camp Sick Quarters, again to a private room. There were two wards for about 50 total, a rarely used Operating Theatre, kitchen etc, catering for about six patients. The relatively large scale was from World War Two, when three-decker bunks had been used in the billets, giving a population of approaching 8,000. A cook was employed for the main meals from Monday to Saturday morning, they came from the Apprentice Mess kitchen at other times.

In charge - at last

After this, unusually, I was detached to Apprentice Wing for disciplinary duties. This detachment was particularly advantageous in two ways. I was excused all Station duties such as Orderly, Fire, Picket and Transit Billet and the corresponding Orderly duties on the Apps Wing were carried out by Apprentice NCOs, under supervision; and were shorter, lighter etc to accommodate their earlier lights-out. Only the Apprentice NCOs in the second year and all third year Apprentices were allowed to wear 'civvies' officially, consisting of blazers, flannels, white shirt and Apprentice tie. Billet checks were carried out frequently to ensure that only those entitled to civvies, had them on camp. To circumvent this, one group cut a trap door in the floor of their hut, excavating down and along underneath it to a larger chamber. It was lined with plywood from tea chests and had electric lighting. They trusted me enough to show it to me.

Regarding discipline in the billets generally, I made it clear that I expected certain standards to be maintained. Reveille was officially 6.30am. Normally, I would get up then, wash, tidy up my room, go to breakfast and return to the billet about 7.15am. The routine then was that as I went through the billet to the ablutions, I would expect to see the majority out of bed, getting dressed etc. When I returned from the ablutions at about 7.20am, every one had to be up. In the evenings, I expected the billet to be quietening about 9.30pm and quiet enough after 10.30pm for those who wanted to sleep, to do so. Officially, the latter time was lights out but if anyone rigged up a small bed-side lamp, they were welcome to do so subject to not annoying any one else. These lamps I expected to be off by midnight.

On Sundays, I insisted that the billets were swept through once, before those who had been off camp returned. The latter had not contributed to the mess, so should not be involved in cleaning up the huge amounts of papers, sweet wrappers etc that always accumulated from Saturday evening onwards.

One Flight Sergeant complained that he never caught anyone in bed in my billets. There was a simple explanation that he was never privy to. In front of the billets was a wide open space. When he was on Orderly duty, he would come marching across there just as I was about to depart for breakfast.

'Good morning, Flight Sergeant Jones' I shouted loudly enough for some of the billet occupants to hear and arouse the rest of them.

Motor vehicles - 2

One Sunday night, I became involved in the aftermath of another motorbike accident. At about 11pm, I had left Margaret, now my wife, in the Nurses' Home and was cycling along the main road to the camp, just past the airfield where the road curves to the left. I noted about six people standing in the middle of the road, a damaged car, a motorbike and two 'bundles' on the road. As I got closer, the bundles turned out to be the motorcyclist and his passenger. Both appeared to be alive; but gave the impression of being seriously injured without there being obvious signs such as blood or angled limbs. One of the group confirmed that the emergency services had been notified. The road was effectively blocked, so I parked my bike and took the battery lamp off it, to wave down vehicles coming from Weston as the road was relatively busy at around that time and the drivers would have little chance of seeing the crash until on top of it. I had stopped about 20 vehicles by the time that the ambulance arrived, which I guided onwards to the crash.

Some 15 minutes later, about 11.45pm, I waved down another car which turned out to be a Police vehicle with a Sergeant driver and three constables. They were from the Somerset Force which had not been notified of the accident yet it was in their area, apparently the Weston Town Police had not notified them. In that era, the Police Forces were organised on a very parochial basis, only some vehicles had HF radios, there were no personal radios. The Sergeant tried to extract a warning sign from the car boot, the only police torch available had the nearest thing to a bent beam that I have ever seen, the batteries being exhausted. I shone my torch into the boot between waving down cars while

Training Times

a Constable took his baton to the recalcitrant sign which was eventually extracted. By this time, I was about quarter of a mile from the crash, so with the sign in position, the Sergeant gave me a lift back to the crash site where we found another Somerset Police patrol with an Inspector in charge. Although we told him that we were not witnesses, he insisted that I and three other RAF bods stay on the scene. At 1.30am, he asked us why we were hanging about, getting upset when we reminded him that he had ordered us to do so; and once more informed him that we were not witnesses.

The two motorcyclists were in the RAF and were returning from London apparently without stopping anywhere. This might not seem particularly dangerous today with the M4 and M5 motorways providing very easy access; but back then, the roads were narrow and twisting. One of the motorcyclists died in Weston Hospital on the Monday. The other was in a critical condition until he also died on the Wednesday. I noted on the Tuesday that one of the airmen in my billet looked rather drawn and asked him if he was feeling alright. His reply was that normally he would have been on the pillion of that motorbike. On the Thursday morning, the Squadron Chiefie asked me to take charge of the funeral details. I explained my involvement, saying that if it was an order, I would carry it out; but would he try to get another NCO to take over. In later years, I have wished that I had carried out the duty.

At work and play

The MPN1 Instructors group normally consisted of two sergeants, three corporals and two civilian instructors. By a combination of circumstances, the group was the only one with an office of its own, Room 40, and was even more privileged to have its own telephone. The other groups, about 40 Instructors and one Admin type, shared one big office upstairs, with one phone. It took a new Admin Sergeant 18 months to find Room 40; and he was surprised to observe the phone as well. Some rapid tales about the importance of our 'specialised' work had to be spun. Due to postings etc, I eventually ended up in charge of the section. As well as the obvious teaching duties, we wrote Air (technical) Publications about the various equipments. Unofficially, we also designed house extensions, got planning consents and organised labour to build them.

We could not draw staplers or hole punches from Stores, typical service bureaucracy; but there were no objections to one of the fitters taking about six weeks to make them! Another example was that when four feet of brass rod was required for a teaching aid, Central Stores issued us with 120 feet. Yet when I carried out a bed inspection in my billets and asked for six replacements, Stores wanted me to hand in the faulty beds for return to Central Stores at Didcot, from which the replacements would come about six weeks later. No one could tell me where the trainees were supposed to sleep in the meantime.

In 1958, the RAF Locking Model Railway Club was started and the club built up quite a large layout in an empty hut behind the NAAFI shop. It was about 30ft x 15ft, OO Gauge; with an additional TT gauge run on one side. I purchased a miniature Minox I 6mm camera which was small enough to place on the tracks between the station platforms. One sergeant was convinced that the resulting photograph was taken at the railway station in his home town. (This camera was the source of about 40 colour slides.)

Civilians at Locking

Generally, the weather in Weston was warmer than I was accustomed to in Edinburgh; but there was one winter when I had to occasionally break icicles off the gears on my bike to allow the derailleur to work. Weston was also wetter; but I noted that the locals only referred to it as raining, never using the range of words such as drizzle, spitting, pouring etc. Although the camp was about two miles inland, it was almost below sea-level. One result was that if autumn high tide coincided with a westerly wind, the sewerage would back up in the toilets; and there was at least one occasion when No 3 Wing was closed down for some days, the occupants getting extra leave. I was subsequently offered and accepted one of the new civilian positions at RAF Locking, going off the camp on Christmas leave in uniform; returning in the New Year, 1961, in civvies, to join a recently-formed section to teach fault finding as a

Training Times

The Old Station Headquarters

subject in its own right. The section had started about 6 months earlier; preparing teaching aids, acquiring samples of various RAF equipments, purloining test equipment in vast quantities from the maintenance stores at RAF Carlisle etc.

The first classes started after the Christmas leave period, graduated to suit the Apprentices involved. The first year Apps experimented with simple battery circuits, working up to designing and 'breadboarding' relatively complex switching circuits. The second year Apps progressed to specially built radios, which could have faulty boards and valves plugged in. For the third year Apps, similar basic radar units were used. The radios and radars including the component boards were made as piece-parts in the School's training workshops, the assembly and wiring being done on a flow-line basis in No 2 Training Block. There were basically 50 radios and 50 radar units made, with many more rigged component boards, faulty valves etc to allow for a wide range of faults.

Goodbye to all that

On 1 April 1961, Margaret and I married in the Church of St David on the edge of Resolven; Margaret having qualified SRN in the January. In the August, when we were on holiday in Edinburgh, I visited Ferranti Dalkeith where I was offered a job in the expanding group that I had started with some four years earlier. I accepted this offer, leaving RAF Locking with many happy memories in November 1961.'

> **The ORB records that in 1960 the Advanced Pt 2 and Direct Entry Fitter's Course required two 'A' Levels - Maths and Physics or a HNC in an appropriate discipline. However, recruiting was failing to match this standard with the consequence that failure rates were causing concern. As a result there was a move to lengthen and re-vamp the course to reflect the need for more academic instruction.**

National Servicemen who were trained at RAF Locking were in general highly qualified and it was not unusual for post nominal qualifications to be used, for example, the corporal's bunk door might have Cpl Bloggs PhD Cambs stencilled on it.

Joe Warn, now living in the United States, was a National Serviceman in the late 1950s who was trained at Locking as a Ground Radar Fitter. Like a lot of National Servicemen selected for training he was a graduate and in the hut there was an established pecking order based on qualification and university, e.g. a Cambridge graduate was above a Durham graduate.

National Servicemen generally did not want to be here and in the main were not happy with the 'boot camp' mentality so all sorts of ways were invented to avoid Sunday Church parades, Joe changed his religion and became the first disciple of the NCCBs - Non Conformist Christian Buddhists and thus, together with other minority groups, avoided

Training Times

Church Parade, much to the Flight Sergeant's chagrin. He also recalls other skives,

'Wednesday afternoon was sports afternoon so a walking club was formed where the only walking involved was to the bus stop for a trip into Weston. Like now there were armed patrols of the Station perimeter, armed with pick axe handles that is, whose job literally was to patrol for two hours and challenge any intruders. However, usually one member patrolled and the other slept in a convenient car. On one occasion on a dark and foggy night a noise was heard and the patrol challenged 'Halt - who goes there?' to which the patrol heard, 'Charlie Chaplain', 'Advance and be Recognised' was the command and the intruder advanced to reveal the RC Chaplain.

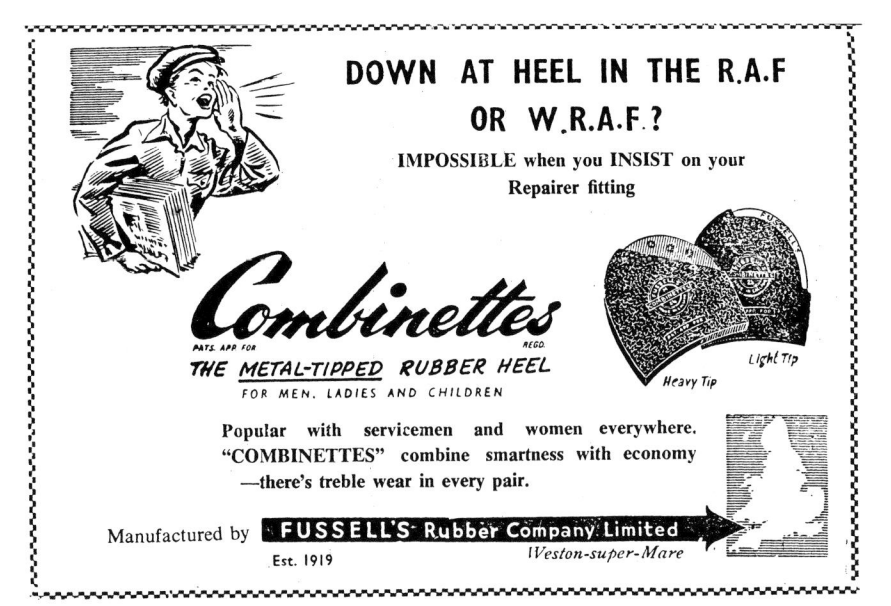

Another feature of life for the graduate entry was that they all built hi-fi systems of one form or another and one serviceman converted two short lockers into a sand filled speaker system complete with bass, mid range and tweeter speakers. Since we avoided church parade, Sunday was the lying in day, however, the guardroom insisted on using that morning for the weekly extended test of the tannoy system which was hard wired to every hut. This upset the electronic boffins so they designed an amplifier system connected to a reel to reel tape deck on which they had recorded spoof messages and tones. This was connected to the tannoy system at random locations by croc clips to confuse and disrupt, not surprisingly the subsequent investigation by the RAF Police of the time failed to find out who was to blame.'

After his National Service Joe joined British Aerospace to work on the Concorde project. In 1967 he was recruited by Boeing for their SST project. He now works in the Nuclear Generating Industry.

Training Times

Peter Gill, a National Serviceman, says he arrived at RAF Locking in November 1957 after completing eight weeks Basic Training at RAF Bridgenorth.

'While we were there, we sat a Trade Test and I became a LAC General Mechanic. I believe the idea was to give us some rank and hence a small additional income, prior to the Radar Fitter trade training, which was about 45 weeks in duration. All the National Servicemen in my group had a HNC or Degree in some technical discipline. In my case a HNC Mechanical Engineering with endorsements and Graduate Membership of the IMechE. I was aged 23 which was typical for those whose entry was deferred to complete their studies. National Service was coming to its end but the pay rates were not sufficient to encourage people with the necessary abilities to sign on for Fitter and Mechanics courses. We had two regular Radar Mechanics on our Ground Radar Course and they had trouble with the mathematics and theoretical parts of the subject matter.

There were, I remember, four Training Squadrons, A and B were for Mechanics Courses and C and D for Fitters. There were large numbers of apprentices on much longer courses than us who shared the training facilities, but we had very little contact with them. About half of our instructors were civilians, the remainder being National Service Corporals who had acquired the necessary skills as part of their professional training prior to enlistment. All my intake covered the same theoretical syllabus which included mathematics up to 'O' level standard, electrical and electronic fundamentals covering everything from Ohm's law to waveguide theory plus practical workshop training. We were split into two groups for equipment training, I was part of the Bendix NPN1 GCA Radar Group and the other half were trained on the CPN4 which was another piece of American equipment, but I can't recall the manufacturer. Our equipment was located at the side of the runway on Weston Airfield and if the wind changed we had to move the two prime mover vehicles, containing the diesel generators together with the trailers containing the living accommodation and the equipment, to the other side of the runway and set everything up before the next aircraft could land! This could take some considerable time on a cold winter's night especially when the diesels refused to start. The CPN4 was also on the airfield but was not required to be moved for a runway change.

We were required to stay on camp on Saturday mornings and were given odd jobs to keep us occupied. The National Service Corporals objected to this as much as we did and the roll call often resembled a scene from a Prisoner of War camp movie. We were usually released at about 11am and most of us headed for home, in my case it was Upminster in Essex a journey of 170 miles. I possessed a 1934 Austin 7 two-seater soft top which was very cold and draughty in the winter. During one trip the crankshaft broke between Newbury and Reading, fortunately there was a garage at Thatcham which specialised in repairing old cars and they installed a new crankshaft ready for collection the next Saturday. Later on, I raided my meagre savings to buy a 1947 Ford Prefect which enabled me to transport three fellow inmates at a £1 per head return to Essex and North London destinations. This was enough to cover the petrol and running costs of the vehicle; I believe we were paid less than £2 per week at the time. Returning to RAF Locking on Sunday nights I handed over the driving following a stop at a 'transport caff' somewhere on the A4 near Chippenham (I still remember the relief when the neon lights of the 'caff' appeared over the hill). Failure to make this stop often resulted in dozing off at the wheel and waking up on the wrong side of the road. On a serious note, there was at least one fatal motorcycle accident while I was at RAF Locking.

The drive back to camp was usually accomplished by 2-3.00am requiring great care to avoid waking the other inmates in the billet. The main problem from lost sleep was that people often dozed during lectures. It was not unusual for unkind people to leave individuals looking conspicuous in an empty classroom, the remainder having moved on to the next lecture. Chuff charts were, and I understand still are, all the rage. We used the

Over and Out 55

Training Times

index 'days done divided by days to do'. This produced an exponential curve which gave considerable encouragement in the final months.

How do I feel now after 40 years? For people like me who had completed their studies it was an interruption to one's career just when beginning to earn a decent salary. I calculated that National Service cost me around £1,200 in lost wages, quite a sum in those days. This lead to some resentment and bad feeling which was no fault of the RAF but rather that of the Government who were only interested in establishing an all Regular Armed Forces rather than considering the woes of the last intakes of the National Servicemen. I think that an 18 year old would have got more out of the character building than we did. On the plus side, there were several people who intended to move into the electronics industry after demobilisation directly as a result of their training at RAF Locking. There was, of course, a good spirit among the National Service inmates and, provided you put any resentment to the back of your mind and just accepted the situation, the two years passed more easily.

Events of the time

• On 29 July 1951 John David Shaw was the first baby christened at St Andrews Church, his parents then living in No 36 Married Quarters.

Baptism and birth certificates

Events of the time

Beach Lawns Exhibition

- On 26 June 1952 RAF Locking hosted the Banwell, Weston and District Agricultural Show which was unfortunately adversely affected by the livestock restrictions in force as a result of Foot and Mouth epidemic.
- On 11 October 1952 a crash of a Vampire on Berrow flats meant that the Station had to provide a crash guard for six days.
- 1953 saw the opening of the RAFA Branch during the Battle of Britain Beach Lawns Exhibition.
- The annual Battle of Britain Parade in Weston, on 20 September 1953, was attended by 250 airmen, 250 cadets and three bands.
- In the 1950s and early 1960s three Varsitys equipped as flying classrooms were operated from Weston airfield to give air experience flights and training to students and cadets, often being flown by qualified aircrew on the staff of No 1 Radio School. On 7 June 1960 WJ 914 collided in flight with a Vampire from RAF Oakington and all eight crew and passengers were killed, included in which were three staff from RAF Locking, one of whom was the pilot.
- On 27 October 1960 there was extensive flooding to the north of the camp which allowed a back up of sewage into the accommodation huts in what is now '8 Area', which required an evacuation for three days until the flood subsided.
- In May 1963 the ORB records that the strength of the Station totalled 2,504:
Officers - 92
Permanent Staff - 625
Airman Trainees - 103
Aircraft Apprentices - 999
Civilians - 417
Attached - 269
- On the 15 July 1963 the 'Binbrook' system of administration was introduced which has largely remained unchanged.

1963 'It was a winter wild' - Milton

Over and Out 57

Fireside WAAFs On Parade

Fireside WAAFS

Who are the girls who appear to be members of the WRAF and yet go home to their mums in the evening? Some call them 'Fireside WAAFs' and others call them 'Uniformed Civilians' but their official title is 'Local Service Women's Royal Air Force'.

In 1959 a scheme was introduced by which WRAF personnel could work at RAF stations near to their homes. RAF Locking was one of the units chosen and in May 1959 a few girls rather apprehensively left Weston for their initial recruit training at RAF Hawkinge (later conducted at RAF Spitalgate). The idea soon caught on and in a short period their strength at RAF Locking had risen to 30.

These airwomen were employed in many areas of the Station on clerical, catering, dental and equipment posts. It was considered that the term 'Fireside WAAF' was somewhat unfairly applied as many girls took full advantage of Service life, taking a full part in Station life and attending evening classes or joining in hobbies clubs.

Most of the sports facilities were open to their participation but fielding teams with only 30 to choose from was difficult at times. Nevertheless, some success was achieved and representative honours were recorded in swimming and three girls formed part of the unit riding team!

Some girls' comments recorded at the time:

On living out: *'Trying to explain to my neighbour that I have not been on leave for the past four years is like trying to collect a travel warrant.'*

On training: *'I have been working for nearly six months and I have got to know all about everything.'*

On SHQ: *'I can still get lost in SHQ if I am not careful and this after 18 months.'*

On male colleagues: *'Some men are rude, others flirtatious and some genuinely pleasant, but these are problems which I will overcome and accept.'*

On marriage: *'In fact it is very common for a WAAF to marry an airman.'*

AFTER ME GIRLS, LET'S SHOW THEM WE CAN MARCH LIKE MEN!

58 *Over and Out*

Cadet Camps

RAF Locking has hosted camps for Air Cadets, mostly ATC, since at least 1949, a practice which has continued unbroken until the present day. Many people who subsequently served at RAF Locking as trainees or permanent staff had their first sight of the camp as cadets. Alex Dow was one of these and his experience is probably typical:

'I joined 142 (2nd City of Edinburgh) Squadron, Air Training Corps, in February 1949. The summer camp that year was at RAF Locking, near Weston-super-Mare. Most of the Edinburgh area Squadrons attended, travelling by special 'troop' train from Edinburgh's Princes Street ('Caley') Station via Carstairs, Carlisle, Stafford (engine change) and Bristol to Locking Road Station. The train was scheduled to leave Edinburgh at 0030 hrs on the Saturday morning with actual departure at 0100 hrs, arriving in Weston-super-Mare about 1530 hrs. From 2100hrs on the Friday evening of school closure for summer holidays, the West End of Edinburgh rapidly became grey/blue in colour as hundreds of cadets converged on the station. The train was 14 coaches long so there was roughly 650 Cadets, Officers and Civilian Instructors on board. It ran out of drinking water early on, unfortunate as the Saturday (and subsequent week) was extremely hot. One of the cadets in our coach had about five pounds of scrap chocolate from Duncan's Chocolate Factory, so we didn't go hungry. *(Rationing of foods, sweets, furniture and clothing continued to about 1953, thus every year, we had to obtain Emergency Food Ration Coupons to cover the period at Summer Camp. We also had to pay an RAF catering fee of four (old) pence per day.)*

RAF lorries and civilian buses took us the four miles to RAF Locking, No 3 Wing, where I had my first encounter with 'real' Service accommodation of the immediate post-war period, typical H-Block huts, three-biscuit mattresses and telescoping beds, the ablutions forming the horizontal of the H. The bedding was issued from another hut possibly 154 of later RAF acquaintance. Our squadron was split between two huts, Nos 164 and 163, next door to the NAAFI. The Mess was at the other end of the row. (I remember the numbers etc as I was based in the same wing during RAF service, about 10 years later.) Being extremely thirsty by then, we rushed to the ablutions for water. It tasted foul in comparison with Edinburgh water.

The RAF NCOs in charge of the huts were PTI's, so we had hectic evenings playing quoits up the middle of the billets, the beds being telescoped to provide more space, followed by hectic 'bulling' of the linoleum. The 'three biscuit' mattresses were effectively mini-mattresses, each about two feet square by three inches thick. When the beds were untelescoped to normal size, each biscuit formed one-third of a full mattress. Every morning, a 'bed-pack' had to be made. First the beds were stripped and telescoped. The three biscuits were placed on top of one another at the head-end. The best blanket was folded thrice length-wise to form a cover, laid flat on the floor initially. The other three blankets and two sheets were folded to a prescribed pattern, then placed on the middle of the cover blanket alternately blanket-sheet-blanket-sheet-blanket. The cover blanket ends were folded up around the pile, one end being tucked into the other end, the result resembling a partially-wrapped liquorice all-sort. The whole bed-pack was then lifted carefully and turned over so that the cover-ends were now lowest, the assembly being place on top of the biscuits with the best folds facing towards the middle line of the hut. After making the bed-packs and generally tidying the hut, the floor had to be polished to get rid of the scratches etc from the previous evening's quoits.

On the Sunday afternoon after Church Parade in the RAF Cinema near the main gate and Fire Station, a group of us decided to go into Weston. We walked about half-a-mile down the main road to the garage at the start of Locking Village, and hired a taxi there, sharing the costs. Ten years later, the same vehicle was still there, a pre-war 21hp, six-cylinder Wolseley.

Classes were held in No 1 Training Block, exposing us to aircraft engines, instruments and the like. RAF Locking was then a training

Cadet Camps

school for adult Regular/National Service airmen recruits. One afternoon was devoted to visiting the Cheddar Gorge and the Wookey Hole Caves where I saw stalactites and stalagmites for the first time. Wednesday Sports afternoon was spent 'howking tatties' for a local farmer.

RAF Locking does not have an airfield of its own, so flying was organised from Weston-super-Mare airfield one mile towards Weston. On the Thursday morning, I went for my first-ever flight, in an Anson, passing over Bristol, Newport and Cardiff. This was no pleasure flight, as we were expected to bring back reports of the members, types and sizes of ships in the respective docks; and in those days, the docks were extensive and packed with ships. It was also my introduction to 'Mae West's' and Parachutes; and the dire consequences of misuse, personal and financial. My main memory of this flight is seeing a milkman delivering to a house in Locking Road, about 500 feet below.

As our hut came second top in the billet inspections, we were considered to have volunteered to work in the kitchens for 24 hours. As I had some cooking and baking experience, along with two other cadets, we worked in the kitchens proper, while the remainder worked in the tin room, vegetable peeling, washing, and drying dishes etc.

The return journey was also by special Troop Train, leaving Weston-super-Mare at 1600hrs on the Friday, arriving at Edinburgh Caley 0930 hrs on the Saturday morning. I slept in one of the luggage racks, bedded down on three greatcoats.'

Alex Dow may be pleased to know that 142 (2nd city of Edinburgh) Squadron ATC is still going strong and in the Summer of 1997 went to RAF Valley for their annual camp. RAF Locking, in the meantime, hosted over 500 cadets over a nine week period this year from five different ATC Wings.

But how much have things really changed in the 48 years since Alex's first camp? Perhaps the first thing he would have noticed had he attended RAF Locking's 1997 annual camps is that camps are much smaller these days - only 60 cadets each week; 30 of which would be girls. Girls were introduced into the Corps in 1980. Our cadets are accommodated in a brick 'T' shaped barrack block, with 15 sharing a large room - each with their own bed space, consisting of a bed, wardrobe, chest of drawers, bedside locker and reading lamp. All the rooms are carpeted and fully centrally heated. Although the cadets are responsible for keeping their accommodation neat and tidy they no longer have to make up bed packs nor are they expected to 'bull' the block - contract cleaners doing the job for them.

Cadets dine in the Airmen's Mess and get their three square meals a day without having to peel a single carrot or pick up a dish cloth or tea towel. During their stay at RAF Locking the cadets follow a full and varied programme of activities, probably much the same as in 1948.

Although Weston-super-Mare airfield is no longer in use, cadets still enjoy air experience flying Bulldog aircraft, operating from 3 AEF at Colerne near Bath. They are provided with an opportunity to fire the cadet version of the L85 weapon and hopefully, get their marksmanship award. RAF Locking is the home of No.1 Radio School and the cadets visit a number of sections around the Station, not to attend classes so much as to see what kind of training RAF technicians undergo and what life in the RAF is all about. The RAF Regiment does, however, teach some skills such as camouflage and concealment techniques which they put into practice on escape and evasion exercise conducted in the Mendip hills.

Cadets also participate in a number of sporting activities, they visit the Fleet Air Arm Museum at Yeovilton, take part in map reading and leadership exercises and go orienteering. The highlight of their week, however, and most probably the activity they will remember the longest, still remains the visit to Cheddar Gorge and Caves. The week ends with a ceremonial parade and march past, with the Station Commander taking the salute, the cadets' general bearing during this parade and the look of pride on their faces amply demonstrates the value that they place on these camps. Clearly the firm foundations set in 1946 by the ATC have proven their worth over the years.

Ceremonial

Each September RAF Locking holds a Church Service and Parade to commemorate the Battle of Britain to remember a battle that was fought and won in 1940.

Battle of Britain Parade passing in front of SHQ

Battle of Britain Parade and Church Service

Battle of Britain Parade 1988 with the Saluting Dias in front of the shops

Some people have always said that we should scrap the memorial service, but the plain fact is that we should always remember the significance of the event since, if the sacrifice of the people that took part in that battle had not been made, the lives of the future generations would have been vastly different, not just for our people but for peoples all over the world.

Over and Out 61

Freedom of Weston Parade

BOROUGH OF WESTON-SUPER-MARE

Dear Group Captain Blair-Oliphant,

Freedom of Entry to the Borough

I am pleased to inform you that the Council, at their Meeting on Monday last, unanimously confirmed a recommendation of the appropriate Committee that a Special Meeting of the Council be convened, on a convenient day to be decided by the Mayor, to confer upon the Royal Air Force Station at Locking, and subject as necessary to the concurrence of the Secretary of State for Air, 'the liberty, honour and distinction of marching through the streets of the borough upon all ceremonial occasions with swords drawn, bayonets fixed, colours flying, drums beating and bands playing.'

I feel sure that you yourself will welcome the proposal and I hope that the Secretary of State for Air will grant his consent to your accepting this honour on behalf of the Station at an appropriate ceremony. I should be grateful if you would kindly arrange for the necessary approach to be made to the Secretary of State so that the preliminary arrangements for the ceremony may be made between us.

After consultation with the Mayor, it is suggested that the ceremony be held on Friday, the 19th October next, commencing in the morning, or if that date should be inconvenient to you, then Friday, the 12th October, would be suitable to the Council.

Your sincerely,
Town Clerk.

Group Captain D.N.K. Blair Oliphant, C.B.E., B.A.,
Officer Commanding No.1 Radio School,
Royal Air Force,
Locking,
Weston-super-Mare

The March Past

Taking the Salute

For the first time, on 12 October 1956, RAF Locking exercised its privilege of marching through Weston-super-Mare with 'swords drawn, bayonets fixed, colours flying, drums beating and band playing'. It did so after the Mayor conferred upon the Station the Freedom of Entry to the Borough.

Bond

Over one year earlier an article had appeared in the 'Mercury' suggesting that RAF Locking be added to the Roll Of Honorary Freeman, as this was the highest honour that could be conferred by the town and that it would serve to strengthen the bond that existed between the Station and town's people.

In the parade was 'No 252 Leading Aircraft Apprentice Ian Bruce Arthur Hamish McCrackers' the brown and white pony mascot. He wore his blue ceremonial suit for the occasion and brought applause as he lead the March Past.

The scroll, which gave freedom of entry into the town, was presented by the Mayor, Mr HJ Holcombe, to the Station Commander Gp Capt DKN Blair-Oliphant in a ceremony in the Town Hall after he had signed the Roll as an Honorary Freeman.

The scroll was in turn handed to the Scroll Bearer who, flanked by two sergeants with bayonets fixed, carried the vellum scroll in a cylindrical transparent case on a tray slung around his neck. He later displayed the scroll to the men on parade in Station Road before it was marched through the town.

In the parade was an escort squadron, composed of permanent staff, who escorted the Queen's Colour of the Royal Air Force, which was being seen for the first time in the West Country. The No 5 Regional Band RAF played as the parade passed by the Saluting Platform. In the parade were the No 1 Apprentice Wing Pipe and Drum Band, No 1 Escort Squadron, No 2 Squadron composed of Airmen Trainees, No 3 Squadron composed of Aircraft Apprentices and the No 5 Regional Band.

Crowds turned out to see the parade and

62 Over and Out

The Scroll is presented to Gp Capt Blair-Oliphant

Signing the Roll

children were let off school early to attend. People filled every vantage point outside the Town Hall where the route was lined by airmen with fixed bayonets. Many shops had special displays and bunting and flags were hung out for the occasion. The Mayor took the salute at the Town Hall as the parade of more than 700 officers and men marched past on a route through the centre of the town. After the parade more than 400 people sat down to a lunch in the Winter Gardens Pavilion.

The Mayor said: *'This is one of those traditions which is truly of significance only in the administration of local affairs. It is a tradition which we are indeed concerned to keep in being because of its direct association with the local democratic institutions of this country - and I may say that it adds to that touch of colour and distinction that we like to have in our local affairs and which in turn does so much to preserve a strong local interest.*

What does this ceremony mean and what is it's significance? It has become customary in this country to honour those who have distinguished themselves in the service of their fellow beings. In the sphere of local government, for the past 70 years, this has been to confer on them the Honorary Freedom of the Borough. Alongside this has developed the practice of conferring the Freedom of Entry as a corresponding recognition of the conspicuous service given by Her Majesty's Armed Forces. This honour, which in these very pleasant circumstances we meet to confer on Royal Air Force Locking, is the highest honour we, as a Borough, can bestow on anyone.'

The Scroll displayed in the Officers' Mess

The resolution moved that 'in recognition and appreciation of the worthy record and services of the Royal Air Force Locking and of their close association with the Borough of Weston-super-Mare to which it is desired to give further encouragement, the Council of the Borough do confer upon the said Royal Air Force Locking the liberty, honour, distinction and freedom for all time of marching through the Borough on ceremonial occasions with swords drawn, bayonets fixed, colours flying, drums beating and bands playing and that the name of the Station be duly inscribed on the Roll of

In Front of the Town Hall in the 1960s

The Parade in the 1980s

Honorary Freemen.'

WO Reid, now retired, has recalled that 'the parade was quite an endurance test because of the distance involved and the fact that the troops were carrying the heavy Lee Enfield rifle and 18" bayonet'.

The Station Mascot

281 'Sparky McDougal', the donkey mascot, was presented to the Station on 23 May 1980 by the Charter Trustees of Weston-super-Mare as a two year old. After completing basic training and passing his 'hay' levels he was promoted to Acting Corporal - unpaid. Twelve years service to the local community followed with hardly a stain on his character, his passing being recorded on numerous roads for all to see! In 1992 the Station Commander, after a 'Gallop' poll, decided to award him a field promotion to Acting Sergeant - still unpaid.

He now resides off station in the care of Mrs Gwen Garfield where he is lovingly cared for, and presented in faultless condition for his many ceremonial duties. Sparky even has his own non public bank account in Accounts Flight and is wealthier than many other areas of the Station.

Handsome

In 1993 the then PRO Flt Lt Sylvia Darby said 'Sgt Sparky McDougal is one of the more handsome members of the Station - and looking after him is a great secondary duty to be saddled with'. Sparky's years of service have, however, not been without incident. He has escaped and chewed his way through the flowers in the Station garden; he was AWOL in 1980 and after being interviewed by the RAF Police, who had no difficulty with the language difference, he admitted the offence on the grounds of wishing to see his girlfriend two fields away. Sparky also got into bother when he was bitten and beaten up by two 'civilians' who were sharing his accommodation. He was quoted as saying 'the civvies were assing around', which resulted in them being banned from the Station.

Sparky's predecessors were

Sparky is promoted

64 *Over and Out*

Hamish in front of the Pipe and Drum Band

252 SAA McCrackers H No 1 Apprentice Wing 1964

Hamish McCrackers, who fronted many Apprentice Passouts, and Heather, both of whom were Shetland Ponies. Heather, who was bought by the apprentices in 1964, retired to a farm in Devon in 1973.

Our 'eathers

LAST YEAR HEATHERS UPKEEP COST £100

The Training of Aircraft Apprentices

(reproduced from 'The Locking Review' 1960)

The purpose of Apprentice Training at RAF Locking is 'to produce advanced tradesmen of good education, and to develop in them such qualities of character, sense of responsibility, leadership and pride of service, as will fit them for a progressive career within the Royal Air Force'.

An Assurance to Parents - Extracted from an Air Ministry Pamphlet:

'A Career as an Apprentice in the Royal Air Force'

To parents

It is natural that parents should wish to be satisfied not only that their son will receive the finest available technical training, but also that his character will develop along the lines they would wish. The term 'Halton trained' has long been accepted as a symbol of all that is best in craftsmanship and in character. Although apprentice training is not now confined to RAF Halton, this tradition, of which we are justly proud, will continue.

Apprentice training in the Royal Air Force is based on long experience of young men. It is designed to give technical tuition second to none, together with character training which keeps pace with increasing maturity. The Royal Air Force apprentice completes his apprenticeship as a skilled craftsman competent to meet the demands of modern technical development and as a responsible and valuable citizen.

The task of teaching and guiding young men is an exacting one, but there is none which gives greater satisfaction. The officers and NCOs at the schools of apprentice training have been carefully selected and there is a wealth of experience from which they can draw. They will be proud to train your boy and are confident you will share their pride in the result.'

The first aim is to produce an advanced tradesman. In everyday terms this means a man who is capable of understanding, maintaining and repairing, where necessary, the electronic equipments which are an

The Training of Aircraft Apprentices

*The Teaching of Radar Maintenance
Time spent on theoretical studies diminishes,
and its place is taken by a practical approach.*

essential part of the operation of the Royal Air Force today. The range of these equipments is so extensive that it is necessary to divide the tradesmen into three distinct trades. These three trades correspond to a division of the function of the electronic equipment; viz., the equipment required for communication purposes, the radar equipments necessary for warning systems and navigational aids, and finally the equipments, communication and radar, which are carried in aircraft.

The task of the Ground Wireless Fitter, is to maintain those receivers and transmitters which are established on the ground for the purpose of keeping in touch with aircraft, the high-powered automatic equipments used in long-distance communication between the Air Ministry and Commands Overseas, the teleprinters which are used in everyday communications systems within the United Kingdom, and the cryptographic machines for ensuring the security of communications. The development of modern radar and warning equipments and radar navigational aids has resulted in the setting up of centres at which are concentrated very complicated and tremendously expensive electronic devices. The training of the Ground Radar Fitter fits him to become the mainstay of maintenance staff at such centres and to understand the working of the transmitters and receivers and their associated display apparatus, as well as the huge aerial equipment which forms an essential part of such systems.

A large part of any military aircraft today is wireless and radar equipment, whose uses vary from the straightforward radio telephone equipment, which enables the pilot to have direct conversation with control points on the ground, to the latest navigational aids. These latter are twofold in type; those which are self-sufficient, and those which are used in conjunction with permanent ground beacon systems.

In order that he shall be capable of installing and maintaining this range of equipment the Air Radio Fitter is trained in the principles of both radio and radar. After gaining a knowledge of the various equipments involved he does have opportunities of trying out such equipment in flying exercises as a significant part of his training.

The responsibilities of the various trades described above is a vast and ever increasing one and the amount of knowledge to be assimilated by the present Apprentice is greater than ever before. The course lasts for three years, and for the young man who undertakes the task it is a hard three years, during which every hour of every working day is fully organised. To complete it, not only ability is required, but also real determination.

In order to understand the method of training it is necessary to emphasise two important

The Training of Aircraft Apprentices

points. The first is to appreciate the nature of the subject. All radio and radar is dependent on electricity, and electricity is something which cannot itself be seen, even though its effects can be deduced or measured. Any explanatory teaching of its behaviour, therefore, is an instructional challenge.

The second fact which needs emphasis is that the training is not limited to a purely factual knowledge of existing equipment. The Royal Air Force is dynamic; the weapons and devices used are continually changing. Each Apprentice must be given a fundamental training which will enable him to follow new developments and techniques as they are introduced.

The first year of the course covers the same ground for all Apprentices, and is largely concerned with classroom and laboratory work. It is intended to extend the knowledge gained in the Secondary Grammar, Technical and Modern Schools, from which Apprentices are drawn, and orientate it in the particular direction required for their future trades. Much time is spent in studying direct and alternating current theory, radio valves and valve circuits. The year is spent largely in studying theoretical subjects, and is, in fact, very much a continuation of school life, but it does lay the foundation on which specialised knowledge will be built.

Theory into Practice

Practising Fault Finding

At the end of this first year of training the division into trades takes place. From this point the training diverges so that attention can be focused on those techniques which are applied to the appropriate equipments. As specialisation begins, attention is directed to the application of techniques to practical devices.

There is, in this second phase, therefore, a gradual transition from theory to practice, and application takes the place of principle. Running parallel to the classroom and laboratory teaching and the knowledge of radio equipment, there is the training in workshops, which teaches the use of hands and tools. Methods of soldering, cable jointing and termination are specialised skills which will be an everyday requirement for these tradesmen. The limited space available for carrying out these tasks in modern electronic equipment demands a highly developed skill of hand.

The final aspect of the practical training is to develop an understanding of how to apply knowledge in a logical fashion to enable a technician to deal with major repairs and modifications, to diagnose and repair faults, to set, tune and adjust the equipments for which he is responsible.

The training described so far is limited to the specific subject matter of the trade. However, training is not limited to the immediate requirements; the second aim is to produce a tradesman of good education. The syllabus, therefore, gives a broad foundation

The Training of Aircraft Apprentices

of knowledge on which to build. This knowledge is not restricted to radio matters, but contains a sufficiency of mathematics to permit a quantitative and analytical approach to the subject and to develop a habit of applying knowledge logically to practical problems. A proportion of each week, during the first year, is devoted to the study of Engineering Science and Engineering Drawing. These subjects are intended as a scientific background to general engineering, and an understanding of how circuits and engineering items can be represented diagrammatically.

The general and cultural studies aspect of the course is devised so that an Apprentice will understand his place in the community as a whole, and the relationship between this country and other countries of the world. To this end there is instruction on the legal and governmental systems of this country, an introduction to world geography, post-war history and current affairs. Many of these matters are dealt with in discussion so that oral and written powers of expression are developed. Each Apprentice, as a culmination of this part of the course, is required to produce an essay, of about 5,000 words, on a subject of his own choice. The subjects chosen are various, and provide an opportunity and training in the acquisition and reproduction of knowledge from a variety of sources.

It is important that training received on the Apprentice Course is recognised outside the Royal Air Force. Apprentices are encouraged to gain civilian qualifications which correspond to their training. The most suitable technical examinations are set by the City and Guilds of London Institute, in Telecommunications Engineering.

In the 1959 examinations 116 Apprentices attacked 221 subjects and were successful in 172 cases, 78 per cent success. Seventeen Apprentices gained the complete Intermediate Certificates of Telecommunications Engineering. Apprentices who arrive at RAF Locking and who have not gained passes in the General Certificate of Education (Ordinary Level) in Mathematics, Engineering Drawing and English are encouraged, provided they are showing satisfactory progress, to gain these. In December 1959, 36 passed in Mathematics, 34 in Engineering Drawing, and five in English Language. A course is now being arranged for outstanding pupils to prepare for Mathematics at Advanced Level in the General Certificate of Education.

To fulfil the third aim of Apprentice training, which is the development of leadership, pride of service and sense of responsibility, instruction is given throughout the course on general service matters. The object is to give an understanding of the Service to which the Apprentice belongs and in which his career will develop and the part that, as a member of that Service, he will play in its military role. At the same time a personal pride in bearing and turnout is produced primarily on the Parade Ground, where the Apprentice is taught how to behave as a member of an organised body of men and also how to control such a body. The peak of this training is seen finally at the Passing Out Parade, when the Passing Out Entry parades under the command of one of its members, for inspection and review by a Senior Air Officer.

Examinations in 3(T)

The Training of Aircraft Apprentices

On Parade in the mid 1960s

The sense of responsibility and leadership is encouraged by the organisation of the domestic life of the Apprentice Wing. Here much of the responsibility for discipline is vested in Apprentice NCOs. These NCOs are responsible to Flight and Squadron Commanders for discipline within the barrack huts and domestic area. Selected for their potential leadership qualities, they are given special privileges, which in turn demand self-discipline over others. It is generally from the ranks of such Apprentice NCOs that will come those fortunate enough to gain Cadetships at the end of the training course.

Sport and physical training are important items in the life of the student. Not only is there the opportunity to play games, but the physical training syllabus teaches the rudiments of all the popular games. As a result many take up sports which, due to lack of facility or lack of knowledge, they have never played before.

The ever popular Model Aircraft Club

One afternoon each week is set aside for games, in addition to the fixtures which are arranged at weekends. Inter-squadron and inter-flight games are played regularly, to add interest for those who find themselves unable to gain places in the teams which compete with other Schools in the Royal Air Force and the Army.

The Locking Society Clubs provide the

Cricket on the Square with 4(T) in the background

The Training of Aircraft Apprentices

opportunities for the development of hobbies such as model-making, photography, amateur radio and printing.

Each year the Apprentices, with help from the instructional staff, produce a full-length variety show.

The Duke of Edinburgh Scheme, with its challenge to youth finds, in the ranks of Apprentices, many who are willing to accept the challenge. Since its inception there has been a high level of response and pursuits and expeditions have been carried out regularly, the latter in some very adverse conditions. Fourteen gold awards have already been gained, and 64 silver awards.

The final hurdle to the training is the Final Trade Test, carried out at the end of nine long terms of preparation by an external examining body charged with the responsibility of ensuring that the correct standards are maintained by the tradesmen of the Royal Air Force. When the final hurdle is overcome and the Apprentice is ready to transfer to the adult Air Force the transition is marked by the Passing Out Parade.

This is more than just a parade it is the last time they will appear in public as Apprentices. As they march off to collect certificates of Apprenticeship and prizes, they become full members of the Royal Air Force and with them go the good wishes of all who have tried for three years to make them as efficient as possible in the part they will play in the future of their chosen Service.

The Apprentice Band

The First Entry to Pass Out at RAF Locking, Air Marshal Sir John Whitworth Jones was the Reviewing Officer

The Wet Weather Parade in 3(T)

70 *Over and Out*

The Locking Apprentice

(Who is this that crawls out from beneath a stone?)

by Sqn Ldr Dick Cheeseman (Retd) 84th Entry 1956-1959
(Reproduced from 'Airwaves' June 1993)

The apprenticeship scheme was well established when it moved from RAF Cranwell to RAF Locking in 1952 and it continued to flavour the character of No. 1 Radio School until it was phased out in the early 1970s. However, the spirit of the apprentice still lives on at RAF Locking as quite a number of civilian instructors and senior RAF personnel were RAF Locking apprentices and will have mixed emotions about those days.

The long sharp shock

'Three years of training - how did we survive? The first year was the hardest; if you survived that you were conditioned to survive for the further two years. There were onerous conditions applied during the first year:
- No civilian clothes to be worn on or off station.
- Only allowed off the station on Saturdays and Sundays from midday until 9.30pm.
- Church parades on Sunday mornings.
- No consumption of alcohol.
- No cars or motorcycles allowed
- If you were a smoker you had to have a smoking pass signed by your parents.
- Part of your pay was compulsorily withheld until you went on leave.
- Lights out was 10pm.

The Entry Spirit

The key to survival was the 'Entry Spirit' which was very strong. We all suffered together, but also banded together to help fellow inmates. There were three entries each year each consisting of 100 to 150 apprentices. Each entry developed its own character throughout the three years training with its own entry banner and song. These came to the fore for sporting and social occasions. For example, for the famous apprentice boxing tournaments we would march from the Apprentice Wing billets (in the area of the present Flowerdown Centre) to the old gymnasium (now Station Workshops) displaying the entry banners and singing the entry songs. The rivalry for the boxing was intense as each entry supported its own champion - I dare not mention that I was in the 84th Entry as no doubt many readers will shout SPROG. They being from the 69th, 72nd or some other more senior entry, such was the spirit.

Power of the Senior Entry

Fear was struck into the hearts and minds of the Junior Entry by the very mention of the phrase 'Senior Entry'. During the last four months of their training the Senior Entry were almost a law unto themselves and had many unwritten privileges. The first experience the Junior Entry had of the Senior Entry was when they were commandeered to clean the Senior Entry billets and bull their kit. You dare not refuse or you would end up with a cold bath. The way to get protection was to volunteer to be a 'kit boy' to a particular member of the Senior Entry and you bulled his kit exclusively. Then there were the raids on the junior billets which happened after lights out when your bed, with you in it, was tipped upside down and your kit taken from your locker and thrown around inside the billet or outside it. This emphasised that your personal kit had to be well marked so it could retrieved more easily.

A 97th Entry Raid on the 101st, AA McKay (now FS) getting ready to clear up

The Locking Apprentice

Once a week the Senior Entry held a kangaroo court in the NAAFI where, once again, the junior billets were invaded and the SPROGS marched off to face such charges as being improperly dressed in the billet. Of course you were always found guilty and had to stand on a table and sing before being released. We longed for the day when we would become Senior Entry.

Saga of the white china mug

Every apprentice had his own mug and 'irons' - knife, fork and spoon for the uninitiated. These had to laid out on the wooden locker for daily inspection as well as being used each meal time. The white china mug barely lasted a week in the first term. During the many kit inspections by the duty NCO he would wipe his finger around the inside of your mug, stand about two inches from your face and with a blast of hot air bellow: 'Dirty, vile, greasy.' SMASH! would go your mug over the iron bed end. After these inspections the billet looked as is a whirlwind had hit it.

Needless to say the NAAFI kept large stocks of white china mugs in anticipation of the frequent whirlwinds.

Another place where your white china mug could disappear was outside the Apprentice Mess in the large hot water trough used for washing mugs and irons after each meal. If you accidentally let go it would sink to the murky depths of this trough never to be seen again. After about 1,000 apprentices had used the trough the contents became quite murky with bits of food floating on the top. We swore that this was used as next days soup although we could never prove it.

Little man - big voice

As you pass the Flowerdown Club there is sign saying 'Parkes Road', which brings back memories of WO Parkes, the Apprentice Wing Warrant Officer. A little man, barely five feet tall, and a former RAF Bantam Weight Boxing Champion. He organised the Apprentice Wing Boxing Tournaments for which he was famous. Parkes Road was his favourite apprentice hunting ground, being small in stature he could hide easily behind a billet or a tree, stepping out just as you were marching down the hill. 'Get those arms swinging shoulder high you flock of docile sheep' he would shout. His voice was heard quite some few seconds before we actually saw him. Apprentices feared him but also respected him at the same time.

Marching to work

Apprentices versus the local lads

Apprentices were always conspicuous in Weston as they always wore uniform. This of course provided bait for the local 'teddy boys' in the 1950s and many a skirmish took place on the beach especially during the summer.

It was the custom of the Senior Entry to leave their mark on the town with such pranks as putting soap powder in the ornamental fountain on the sea front or hoisting the Entry Flag on top of the Odeon Cinema.

Good guys - bad guys

Good conduct stripes were awarded if your crimes went undetected, these were worn at the bottom of the left sleeve of your uniform. By the time you had reached your final two terms the apprentice had accumulated three of these stripes.

After the first year certain apprentices were selected to hold a local NCO rank to give them additional responsibility at a young age. A leading apprentice (one stripe) would be responsible for one billet of 22 apprentices, a corporal apprentice would have charge of two billets and live in a bunk at the end of one of them - what luxury. A sergeant apprentice would be responsible for a squadron - approximately 450 apprentices. The flight sergeant apprentice was selected for the passing out parade only. At 1000hrs the next day we would all be demoted to junior technicians for real and be away on our postings.

The Locking Apprentice
Sacred ground

This of course was the parade square used exclusively for parades and drill instruction and was out of bounds at all other times. This was the territory of the Station Warrant Officer and he could often be seen stalking the perimeter like a game warden looking for poachers. In those days car parking was never a problem since, as apprentices, we never had cars.

The first year of the apprenticeship included a very large dose of initial training - that meant plenty of drill. For my entry that meant an extra large dose to get ready for the inaugural Freedom of Weston Parade in 1956. As we always wore studded boots, drill timing could be more precise and we could hear our movements, compared to today's soft shoe shuffle.

The frequent parades were always lead by the Apprentice Wing Pipe and Drum Band with the Shetland Pony Mascot, 'Hamish McCrackers', who held the rank of Leading Apprentice.

These days when I come through the gate I expect to see the guards in red jackets and white trousers giving a cheery 'Hi-De-Hi' welcome to the RAF Locking Holiday Camp. Yes, times have changed and I must change with them.

At the end of the day taking everything into consideration I am proud to say, 'yes, I was a Locking Apprentice and wouldn't have missed the experience for the world.'

Now I can crawl back under my stone.

Hamish and the Pipe and Drum Band at a Passing Out Parade

(Hamish McCrackers later advanced in rank to Corporal Apprentice and on a number of occasions disgraced himself, once breaking out of bounds and eating the flowers in the Station Garden, for which he was charged). Apprentice Wing being about a thousand strong could fill the parade square with its three squadrons.

The Station Layout in 1964

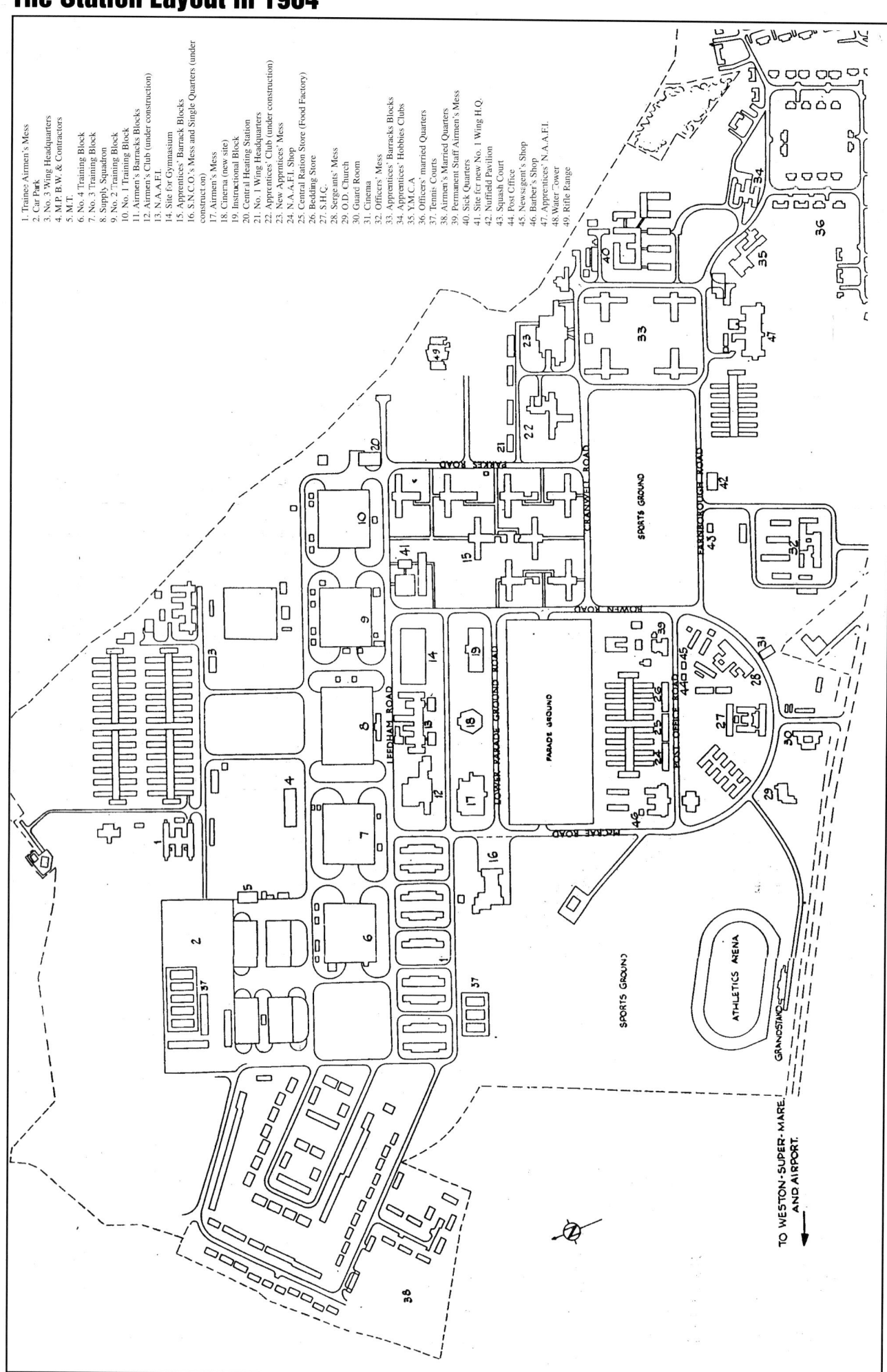

1. Trainee Airmen's Mess
2. Car Park
3. No. 3 Wing Headquarters
4. M.P. B.W. & Contractors
5. M.T.
6. No. 4 Training Block
7. No. 3 Training Block
8. Supply Squadron
9. No. 2 Training Block
10. No. 1 Training Block
11. Airmen's Barracks Blocks
12. Airmen's Club (under construction)
13. N.A.A.F.I.
14. Site for Gymnasium
15. Apprentices' Barrack Blocks
16. S.N.C.O.'s Mess and Single Quarters (under construction)
17. Airmen's Mess
18. Cinema (new site)
19. Instructional Block
20. Central Heating Station
21. No. 1 Wing Headquarters
22. Apprentices' Club (under construction)
23. New Apprentices' Mess
24. N.A.A.F.I. Shop
25. Central Ration Store (Food Factory)
26. Bedding Store
27. S.H.Q.
28. Sergeants' Mess
29. O.D. Church
30. Guard Room
31. Cinema
32. Officers' Mess
33. Apprentices' Barracks Blocks
34. Apprentices' Hobbies Clubs
35. Y.M.C.A.
36. Officers' married Quarters
37. Tennis Courts
38. Airmen's Married Quarters
39. Permanent Staff Airmen's Mess
40. Sick Quarters
41. Site for new No. 1 Wing H.Q.
42. Nuffield Pavilion
43. Post Office
44. Post Office
45. Newsagent's Shop
46. Barber's Shop
47. Apprentices' N.A.A.F.I.
48. Water Tower
49. Rifle Range

74 *Over and Out*

'Ye General Salute - Present Ye Your Pikes'

An ancient document in Norman-English came to light during repair work on the foundation posts of the Station Headquarters in the late 1950s, on the site of the old keep of Castle Locking (AD 1025). The translators in No 3 Apprentice Wing have endeavoured to maintain the vigour and polish of the original Saxon-Norman language while rendering it comprehensible to the modern reader:

Once upon a month in the morne of Saturne
Following in a righte regulare patterne
By the juste order of oure Castle Commander
We holde a righte merrie Military philander

From Castle Keep quarters the news starts its travilling
And ye erks in the Courteyard do take up their cavilling
But a stop is soon placed for to curbe their gurlling
By gallante Lords Ackrille, Linnarde and Stirling

Each stoute retainer with tweye hauberks is kitted
And his nombre one chainmail is anon duraglitted
And worthi Knights, ye court's crack riders
Hie to the heerdresser, for ye shorte back and siders

And so to the morne, everichon rises righte earlie
To partake in the occasion teat cometh twelve yearlie
Yea, everichon into yea courtyarde doth enter
Ye Baron hath bidden a hundred per center

We steppe into place to sackful andante
They are proven moste justely by ye parade Adjutante
Dom Linnarde doth appear, lest our minds meander
And thus we receive our Baron Commander

Our accroutrements are given a fortheet inspection
To ensure that ye hinges are oiled to perfection
And if any pike hath some rust camouflaged
Ye bold Sheriff shall see that he's charged

And so we manoeuvre by echelons in columne
Sphering oure orbes in an een right moste solemne
Passing yon high plinthe of loyal salutation
Stepping to ye Pipe and Drum modulation

So we warriors of Britain, ye airmen divers
Ye apps and ye mechs and all parade skivers
When thinking conditions of service are shocking
Reflect on youre forbears at Ye Castle Locking

The 71st Entry (1952 - 55)

The 71st Entry arrived on 30 April 1952 as the first entry of apprentices to be-gin their course at RAF Locking and were known as a detachment of No 6 Radio School RAF Cranwell.

A straggling bunch of civilians already with signs of doubt about RAF life were greeted at the railway station by a perfect example of a drill instructor, who rather frightened us at the time. On arrival at RAF Locking we were shown our billets and then conducted to our first meal (no comment) with questioning glances at each other.

The first week passed with the usual medical examinations and initiation ceremonies not forgetting instruction on 'bulling', shining billet floors and folding blankets.

Also in this week we received our full kit which was found to be too small for the tall apprentices and too big for the short ones. Then of course came drill periods between lectures and showers of rain, and we began to consider ourselves apprentices, a fact soon dispelled when we commenced technical training in temporary accommodation as the sheds were not then ready for use.

Mike (Ernie) Fiske, 587748, recalls:

'The most wonderful Christmas Dinner in 1952 that I had ever seen or eaten. It was the

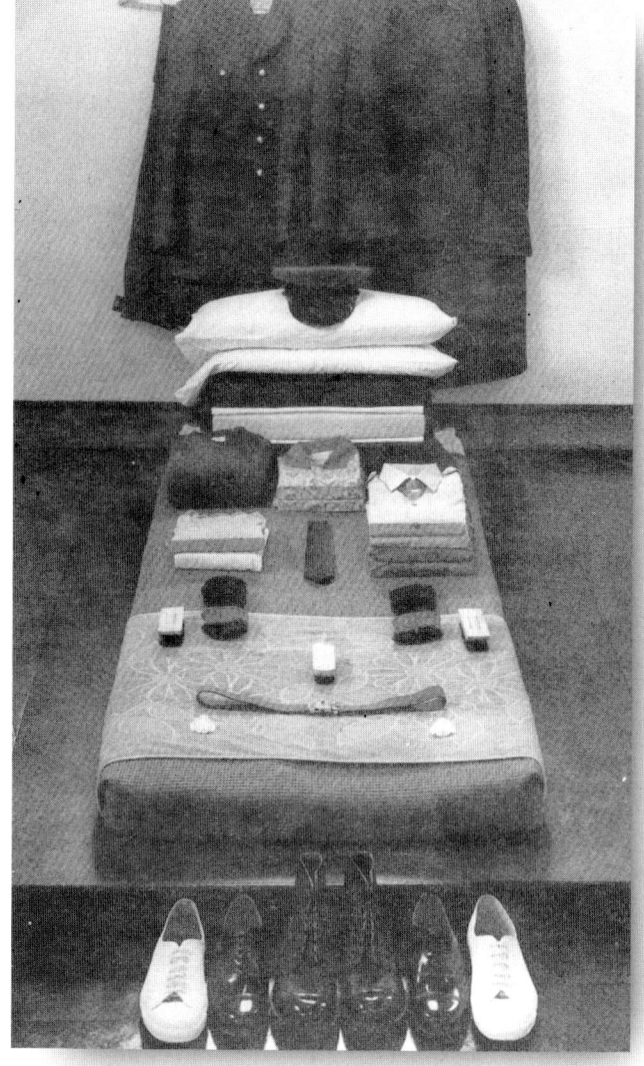

The Blanket Pack

first time that I had ever tasted turkey and to be able to smoke a fag without being asked to show a 'smoking pass' was a rare event to be enjoyed (they even supplied the fags)

The Station Pig Farm and the time someone moved the Station Commander's Residence sign to the entrance to the farm. I suspect that Gp Capt Monks was not amused - but we were.

The night Charlie Chester put on a show - and the padre had the stripper cancelled. He was worried that the young boys would have a crises of morality - he obviously didn't know how wicked was the Aircraft Apprentice when in tribal pack'.

Christmas Dinner in 1958

The 73rd Entry

On 21 January 1953, 75 boys arrived at RAF Locking to commence training as Aircraft Apprentices. Barely one hour after arrival we were officially signed on and we took the oath. A certain corporal, well known among the apprentices, then marched us away for our first of many haircuts.

The following day we were marched to clothing stores and issued with our complete kit and for the rest of the day we were engaged in removing the unwanted creases from our uniforms and inserting creases where they should be. The same evening we were introduced to the delights of bulling by former boy entrants. In the days to come the self same corporal introduced us to the pastime of drill and he told us that we were the worst entry that he had ever met. This made us somewhat crestfallen until we found out later from more senior apprentices that he said that to everyone. At this time we also had lectures about Service life and what was expected of us as apprentices.

Technical training started on 9 February and by the end of that term we had completed DC Theory and Magnetism. Everyone did well in the examinations and on 27 March we were all pleased to be released for 12 days leave.

Going on leave at Weston Railway Station

The 74th Entry

We arrived in twos and threes on 29 April 1953, although the two New Zealanders and three Ceylonese had already settled in. As soon as we entered the camp we were met by grinning apprentices who warned us not to sign on, but we lightheartedly signed our papers. Upon entering our accommodation we all suddenly realised that we had lost part of our freedom.

We managed to survive the hut inspections and domestic nights overseen by a Leading Aircraft Apprentice and even the activities of the 'Ramsgate Tyrant' on the Parade Square became bearable. The majority of us initially felt homesick but only one of our number bought himself out.

Although we laugh at it now we were all

Relaxation and Writing Home

affected by the inoculations and in fact in those same few days three of the entry went sick with appendicitis, but how that relates to the jabs is anyone's guess. After we started technical training we counted the days to the Whitsun Grant, however, our leave was delayed a week because we were dedicated to route lining for the visit of HRH The Princess Margaret.

One very annoying factor at this time was that we kept having to change billets - but what more could we expect from the RAF?!

On 15 July half the entry went to RAF Odiham to watch the Coronation Review of the Royal Air Force by Her Majesty the Queen.

The weekend before the first summer leave saw the first of our number to be charged and confined to camp for three days. Finally, just before the end of term we witnessed our first Passing Out Parade - that of the 66th Entry.'

Over and Out 77

Apprentice memories

Dixon of Dock Green

Mr Jack Warner and the company, the cast of the weekly television series, 'Dixon of Dock Green', together with the producer and technicians, visited the Station on 17 February 1958 to film shots of a Passing Out Parade which included a youth actor in the company.

The sequence was to form a sequel to an episode televised on 1 March 1958 on the theme of a 'boy making good'. The company was entertained in the Officers' Mess and the piece was then filmed, the 82nd Entry having the honour of performing.

Robin White, ex of the 86th Entry, now Squadron Chaplain of the ATC recalls the winter of 1957 which was cold and was also the first away from home for the then 15 year old apprentices. With little money, and always hungry, Tuesday to Thursday evenings were miserable. He recalls:

'On one particular cold and miserable day after the morning Wing Parade on the snow covered square, the lads in our billet were cheesed off at the prospect of having to spend an evening in the billet because we could not afford to go to the NAAFI.

After discussing many ways of raising money, including selling Ginger Thompson into white slavery with the 83rd, the ideas were getting ever more far fetched with little progress. Why don't we cook supper for ourselves in the billet, I suggested. The plan was that each apprentice would bring back from the mess after tea something that could contribute towards supper for the 20 of us in the billet. Later in the evening we would commandeer the ironing room and assemble all the electric irons we could muster from around the flight lines to use as cookers.

Versatility

Thanks to the versatility of RAF coveralls with their many and various pockets an intriguing array of supper ingredients duly appeared. Loaves of bread, margarine, jam, tea, sugar, evaporated milk and several skins of sausage meat, which seemed to be made to measure for the outside leg pocket of the overalls.

A foraging party was sent out to collect the irons and to go to the back of the Mess to find a used pomme (instant potato powder) tin. All was now set to cook supper for 20 on four electric irons.

The ironing room with its four large wooden tables was ideal as a kitchen. Soon a production line was set up; one lad sliced the sausage on the first table into flat round patties (beef burgers were unknown then) and placed them onto an upturned iron held by the second lad. The bottom of the iron had been greased with margarine by a third cook, and when the pattie was placed on the iron a second iron was placed on top to cook both sides at once.

Meanwhile on the second table the toast was being prepared be another team by the simple expedient of ironing each slice of bread with an iron turned up to its highest setting. The toast was then passed to the third table where it was margarined and passed to the fourth table to await the pattie.

Cooked patties were assembled on the fourth table and then hurried by a team of runners down the billet for distribution to the rest of the hungry apprentices. After the sausage meat toasts had been eaten, augmented by the remaining bread, marg and jam, there came the question of tea.

The empty pomme tin was filled with water and hot irons pushed firmly onto each side until the water boiled, a handful of tea leaves and milk were added and the whole lot shaken, not stirred. Placing several RAF issue socks on his hands the tea boy carried the boiling hot tin to the others who were waiting at the foot of their beds with mugs in hand. He was preceded by one person who was armed with a bumper pad to catch the drips and a freshly laundered handkerchief to act as a strainer. With sugar added and a handful of sultanas, courtesy of an open barrel in the store room next to the plate wash, the supper was declared to be the best ever.'

78 *Over and Out*

Apprentice memories

Phil Mills is the Secretary of the 90th Entry Apprentices Association and he has provided a number of anecdotal tales based on his own experiences and on those of his association's members:

'Remember the summer of 1961, many will because it was a lovely time to be a member of the Senior Entry at RAF Locking. There was something quite challenging about defying the odds and illegally crawling out of the camp through the hole in the hedge behind the Officer's Mess, to escape to the Brewer's Arms in Banwell, or somewhere else out of bounds for two or three pints and a game of darts. In those days we could get blissfully blotto on three pints of scrumpy for half a crown. The lucky few of us with motorbikes in handy secret hideaways near the camp, roared away with pillion passengers hanging on for dear life to places further afield, like Draycott to do a bit of strawberry picking, to get a few bob to spend at the Strawberry Inn afterwards.

Talking of the Strawberry Inn - It was a week or two after the 1961 Draycott Strawberry Fare, after chucking out time at the Strawberry Inn, when some gallant merry makers of the 90th Entry were leaving the pub. They were hailed by an attractive young lady leaning out of her bedroom window. 'Here, you boys, will ee do something for me?' The pleading by such a damsel just couldn't be ignored. Her father had locked her in the bedroom because she wanted to elope with her boyfriend. While we were talking to her the father came out and told us to, 'mind your own business and go away in short jerky movements'. But the pleas of his broken-hearted daughter were rather like a call of nature - it just had to be answered. The father got more than he bargained for, he was tied to a chair, his daughter released, who was last seen driving of on a tractor with her boyfriend towards Cheddar.

Remember FS Beetell? We called him 'Beetle'. He didn't like the 90th - he was in the wrong squadron. He always seemed to turn up at the wrong time, one moment the coast was clear, the next Beetle appeared on his bike. Beetle and his bike were an item as we rarely saw him off it, but one day we did. He was spied going into a B Squadron hut and he left his bike where it could be pinched - and pinched it was. It was next spotted during the following morning's NAAFI break suspended high above the apprentices' heads in the middle of the indoor parade ground. How on earth Beetle's bike was ever suspended from so high up in the roof structure of 3(T) was a real mystery, because it took special equipment to retrieve it later.

Talking about Flight Sergeants - Ted Pollard was Duty Sergeant one night. He was checking on the guard and was stood beneath the water tower having a quiet five minutes and a fag when he heard a little sound from above. Shining his torch he saw looking down at him one of his apprentices - Curly Cambelton with a entry flag in his hands. Curly was dangling upside down over the side at the top of the water tower held by his ankles by two of his compatriots, unseen from below. 'It's OK Chief' whispered Curly 'you finish your fag - I'll be done in a tick'. The entry flag remained in place for two days before being removed.

'In those days we could get blissfully blotto on three pints of scrumpy for half a crown.'

When the old huts were being demolished the workmen put all the old toilet pans to one side to be taken away later - and they made a second mistake by leaving sand and cement around, too.

It was getting close to passing out time and every parade had a rehearsal. On the parade square everything was in order, all the spots were marked for the markers and flight commanders. What fun it would be, we thought, to mark the spots with something everyone would see - but with what?

Toilet Pans was the answer! Four of us busied ourselves under cover of darkness - two taking toilet pans to the parade square, one mixing mortar and the other keeping cavy. Heavy stuff mortar, heavier than toilet pans, but we stuck at it and eventually everything was assembled. On the parade square over each marker spot a toilet pan was set into a good dollop of cement. On the dais were set three toilet pans, one each for the

Apprentice memories

Commandant, his Adjutant and the stand-in Reviewing Officer.

The next morning the Apprentice Wing assembled on time for the passing out rehearsal. Suddenly as the junior entries were about to march off the Wing Warrant Officer began to do his nut at the Parade Square. All hell was let loose, he was shouting at people and bawling left, right and centre. The junior entries marched on 40 minutes late. Being the senior entry we marched on last. The Wing Warrant Officer stood at the marching on point with a face like thunder. There wasn't a toilet pan to be seen anywhere, just a lot of dirty wet patches and no nice marked out spots.

Nothing was ever said about the incident afterwards, but someone found another use for the toilet pans. They appeared on the top of 2(T), all beautifully lined up as if on parade with a big banner underneath proclaiming:

'Abandon hope all ye who enter here'

Then there was the night when we held a midnight parade rehearsal. Bulled up to the eyeballs - pyjamas, gleaming hob nailed boots and brasses, rifles and white webbing. We got the smallest apprentice from the junior entry to take the salute and then marched off with rifles at the slope and fixed bayonets through the Officer's Married Quarters. They were all in bed and we woke everyone up - except our flight commander - Ted Edwards. Someone else rang him just to tell him, 'your bastards are at it again.' Ted watched us march past his house from behind his bedroom curtain, half expecting an angry call from the Commandant, which never came.

We had some fun with Ted. He came round on a bull night and while he was inside we put his new Mini on a foot high concrete plinth some workmen had just constructed. And who remembers how many balloons we blew up to cram C Squadron offices so full that Ted and the others had difficulty in opening the doors the next day, let alone get into the offices?

Who remembers the ghost of the headless airman who walked from the Apprentice's NAAFI to Sick Quarters, via the junior entry billet? Frightened the poor little dears out of their wits apparently.

And then there was the World War Two mine!...

In the summer of 1960 the 90th Entry went to Penhale Sands, near Newquay on summer camp. On the sea front was a mine painted red to collect donations for the RNLI. When the two weeks were up, the 90th Entry returned to RAF Locking and the 91st Entry went to Penhale. The red mine was still there, but not for long. Whether it was a combined entry effort is not clear, but some form of illegally obtained transport was used to move the mine from Newquay to a secret location near to, or on the camp.

In those days there was a rostrum for a policeman to direct traffic at a busy junction in Weston (High Street and Regent Street - Burton's Corner). Very early one morning a few of the 90th and 91st entries took the mine to Weston on a cart and placed it on the rostrum. The local coppers soon discovered it and their suspicions were soon aroused by a group of young men seen on the road near Weston Airport with a sturdy cart running in the direction of the camp. The long and short of it was when challenged they owned up and were made to return to Weston and remove the mine. It is said that the mine decorated a farmer's muck heap for some time, and then disappeared - only to turn up again months later.'

NAAFI Provided Many Services

NAAFI and YOU

"Food for thought"...

R.A.F. Dishforth and R.A.O.C. Donnington. These were the stations originally selected for an experiment which could revolutionise Service catering.

Naafi was given the entire responsibility for providing, cooking and serving all the meals for officers, senior N.C.O's. and men at both places.

The quality and variety of the food and the general standard of the service continue to receive high praise from all ranks.

The success of the experiment has resulted in Naafi's contract being extended to other military establishments.

IMPERIAL COURT, KENNINGTON LANE, LONDON, S.E.11
H.M. Forces' Official Trading Organisation   Another example of Naafi's Service to the Services.

Apprentice memories

More on the mine saga from JM Moore, 684850, who was not involved in the recovery which he says involved overnight journeys the length of the West Country in illegal cars, double dealing on sprog entries and all manner of underhand goings on. However, he clearly was involved in subsequent events:

'My involvement with the thing began late one Saturday evening in the spring of 1961. When I first met it, it was lying in the middle of a manure heap just around the back of Locking Village. I, and about a score of other 90th Entry had collected there with a view to manoeuvring it onto the squadron handcart. It was a fine handcart, all metal with large car wheels and sturdy handles. Its quality was, I suppose, our ultimate undoing.

By midnight it was safely aboard the trolley and we set off for Weston at a good pace, with half the team in harness and the other half ready to take over from anyone feeling the effects of too much scrumpy from earlier in the evening.

We passed the Borough Arms without incident and the streets were deserted as we proceeded on our way. Even though we were all shod in plimsolls, our passing had not gone unnoticed for it was not long before we met a detachment of the local constabulary.

Convinced

One of our number, whose silver tongue should, by now, have elevated him to at least cabinet level, convinced the police that mine was destined for an officer's front garden in Worle. With a conspiratorial chuckle and a 'Good wheeze lads' we were bade on our way.

At the confluence of the five roads in Weston the rostrum was quite unique. About four feet in diameter and two feet six high with a little parapet another foot high running around it, it seemed the ideal place to locate the mine. It was the work of a moment for 20 strapping lads to off-load the mine onto the rostrum, which we achieved by 2.15am.

And then we made our first, and terminal, mistake. Actually it was more of a compound error, since we decided not to abandon the cart, split up and make for camp in twos and threes via the back streets and fields. Instead, it seemed a better idea to leg it, in formation, complete with handcart, straight up the main road, directly to Locking. At 3.30am, just as we approached the airfield straight, and with the camp so tantalisingly close, the long arm, or rather, the fast patrol car, of the police finally caught up with us. The police had outwitted us!

It was about turn and back to Weston, accompanied by the police car, a bus complete with camp guards, the Duty Officer and a Snowdrop. We retrieved the mine by about 4.45am and recommenced the long haul back to camp arriving by 6.30am or so. We were all charged, did janks, which should have been the end of the incident. It probably was for everybody else.

> *'At the confluence of the five roads in Weston the rostrum was quite unique. About four feet in diameter and two feet six high with a little parapet another foot high running around it, it seemed the ideal place to locate the mine. It was the work of a moment to off-load the mine onto the rostrum, which we achieved by 2.15am.'*

On passing out I was posted to RAF Sealand, which was strange camp with more civilians than airmen. In fact, there were only sufficient airmen to fill one 16 man room, so we all knew each other. Occupying a pit fairly close to me was a most objectionable National Serviceman who insisted on telling me several times a day what he thought of apprentices. Not being renowned for my tolerance or good grace, I sustained his jibes for a few days before I had enough and rounded on him:

'Look, just what is you problem, cause we can settle this outside here and now if you like.'

'No no' he said, 'it's just that when I was at Locking a few months ago a bunch of stupid apprentices put a mine on the copper's rostrum in Weston and I was on guard that night and spent half of it rounding them up. It's nothing personal.'

But it was.'

Apprentice memories

Mike Furness recalls other japes:

'All the signs on all the buildings were screwed to the walls with one inch wooden screws which were easy to remove and reinstall in the dark, in a different location of course. I recall taking great pains to place the sign 'Bulk Ration Store' on our 'large' flight commander's door. Also, during one night, we bricked up the doorway to the squadron office using bricks and mortar which had been purloined from the builders working on the new accommodation. I am not sure now how we managed it in so short a time, I certainly could not do it now.'

Paul Tuffrey was also of the 90th Entry:

'Who will forget the Apprentice Mess? Those long queues of hungry apprentices waiting to have food unceremoniously dumped on their plates by bored duty junior apprentice servers and the after meal ordeal of washing one's irons and china mug in a tank of boiling water without being scalded in the attempt. One lost count of the number of irons that slipped through the mesh of the rinsing basket to be lost forever beneath the bubbles of rising steam.

Greasy Joe

The cooks that catered for the apprentice wing seem to have been chosen for their belligerence rather than for their catering skills. Who will forget the corporal cook, Greasy Joe, whose oily features always seemed to be as unwashed as the splattered cook's uniform that he always wore. I remember one poor apprentice who had the temerity one morning to ask him for a boiled egg.

'Who the 'ell do you think you are?' shouted Joe, 'you can have fried egg or scrambled egg like everyone else - boiled egg never'.

After a few days of this the apprentice not to be beaten, broke into the Mess one dark night and boiled every egg in sight! The look on Greasy Joe's face the following day as he tried to crack tray after tray of pre-boiled eggs was a joy to behold.

In comparison, the civvy members of the Mess were delightful and in our senior year, ensured that our illicit late breakfast club was always provided with freshly cooked eggs and bacon.

Despite our frequent requests, the coke machine was never moved outside the Mess which resulted in many a late night break in just to put one's money in the slot and sneak out with an armful of orders. Ever time I passed the guardroom and saw the 'guilty' doing their jankers I used to think 'there but for good fortune!'

Summer Camp

An undoubted highlight (although not appreciated by all) was the Summer Camp at Penhale Sands where for a week we slept under canvas and played at being boy soldiers. The mock battle where opposing Red and Blue teams fired blank ammunition and threw thunderflashes at each other was taken extremely seriously by our Rock Ape mentors. They were definitely not amused when Tony Cotter although 'eliminated' and out of ammo continued to aim his gun at the opposing team shouting out in his cultured voice 'Bang! Bang!' every time he pulled the trigger. The cross-country trek was also an experience not to be forgotten. After stumbling across crater-filled fields our team decided to take a 'short cut' along a railway line. I will always remember the astonished looks on the faces of the people on the platform as we marched up the platform ramp, along the platform and disappeared into a tunnel at the other end leaving the refrains of our rugby songs hanging in the air.

Senior Entries

In the days that we joined the apprentices as young sprogs, the senior entries ruled the roost and No. 1 Radio Training School suffered the worse excesses of 'Tom Brown's School Days'. We were expected to shout 'Senior man present' and jump to attention whenever a Senior Entry apprentice entered the billet. In addition we were subjected to Senior Entry full kit inspections where the inspected sprog could expect to have dust smeared on his face and his kit thrown about while being subjected to verbal abuse. You considered yourself lucky if all that was found was a 'spot' on your china mug which resulted in it being smashed on the bottom rail of your bedstead. Fagging was considered the norm and fags, on being summoned to a Senior Entry billet, were expected to salute whatever passed as a mascot (usually positioned above the tannoy speaker) as they entered the door. To fall foul of a Senior Entry member was to invite disaster for kangaroo courts were held to judge 'offenders' and mete out bizarre punishments. Even the NAAFI was no escape as one could be dragged into the 'Senior Entry Only' room and be forced to stand on the table and sing a song amidst a great deal of barracking.

What proved to be the final straw for the 90th was the perpetual night raiding which resulted in individuals being dragged from their beds (pits) and suffering other forms of harassment including being asked if one wanted to buy a battleship! Enough was enough and the 90th retaliated and raided the Senior Entry; the first Junior Entry in all of Locking's history to have the guts to do so. Retribution from the Senior Entries came swiftly. We were in the NAAFI at the time and wondered what the crashing noise could mean. We soon found out. Our billets were totally wrecked, our highly polished floors ruined by hob nail boots and bicycles and our beds dismantled and thrown about. Some unfortunate members of the 90th were still on the roofs of the huts recovering bits of their beds long after midnight. Still we had made out point and as far as I can remember we were never raided again.

Come the end of term, we were marched en masse to 2T block where we queued up for hours for train passes to our home towns before being put on buses to Weston-super-Mare Railway Station. Once there, we were herded on to special trains. It was a major operation that none of us appreciated. It was not uncommon to see apprentices who had made other holiday arrangements make a rapid escape from the non-platform side of the train and disappear over the tracks. On one occasion a group of escaping apprentices hid in a solitary stationary carriage which to their dismay was coupled up and ended up in Patchway.

Drill Instructors

'Beetle' wasn't the only DI to end up with an aerial bike. Remember Linus the Irish DI whose accent was so thick that it was difficult to understand him? He was one of nature's least loveable characters and the more he was wound up the less intelligible he became. We obtained much pleasure in 'misinterpreting' his commands on the parade square and delighted in the resulting chaos. His bike ended up one night 'flying' from the overhead heating pipe by the NAAFI.

'Arms' Pollard was famous for the length of his limbs and one Christmas the 90th presented him with a double-arm RAF pullover!

One day 'Flapper' Atkinson inconsiderately blocked the road by commanding our junior entry to open order as I was approaching on my bike. Not to be deterred, I continued on my way and cycled right through the flight. 'Flapper' went berserk and for a moment I thought he was going to have a seizure. 'Bbbbb******y 90th… R-r-r-r-r-report t-t-t-t-to me tomorrow morning. I'll p-p-put you on a fizzer' he stammered. I duly reported but fortunately he failed to turn up!

Padres

To save our souls, Locking provided a variety of Padres whose backgrounds were as varied as the churches they represented. By far the most colourful was Padre Schofield an ex-professional magician who could always be counted on to put on a good show at our YMCA Christmas concert. He was famous for using a ventriloquist dummy in his children's sermons.

Apprentice memories

This practice incensed a member of his civilian flock who sent him a letter accusing him of being the 'son of the devil'. Schofield took mischievous delight in promptly mailing a response commencing 'Dear Father......'

Church clubs too provided an ideal way to meet apprentice seeking teenage daughters from married quarters. This served to satisfy two desires - the first of winning female companionship, the second, the chance of an invite home and 'feet under the table' for Sunday lunch. The latter was often the most favoured objective.

Cars and Motorbikes

I will never understand why it was illegal for apprentices to own cars and motorbikes once they'd reached the national qualifying age. Perhaps they were afraid of us all driving off never to return. Despite the ban, vehicles were stashed away. John Gray had a superb Wolsley garaged in Weston while Tony Petter garaged his Standard Ensign in the 'Boggies' (National Service) Wing right on the base! Many a night we drove up and down 'Skid Row' while I took my first driving lessons without even leaving the camp-wonderful!

Finally, it was all a long time ago since we burnt our boots (to obtain a good shine), burnished our cap badges on the back of mats, slithered about with squares of blankets on our feet (to keep the linoleum gleaming) and starched (some even sewed) creases in our uniforms. It must all seem a bit bizarre to today's airmen (who probably wouldn't know a 'housewife' or a 'button-stick' if they saw one).

Nevertheless, as we swung our bumpers to the Everly Brothers', 'wake up little Suzie' and Presley's 'I wanna be free' we shared a lot of experiences (and very often the same suit). This and the high standard of technical training we received stood us in good stead later on. Looking back it's amazing how much we packed into those three years and the bond forged between us kept us together in later service and long after - especially during the famous 65 Squadron 'work-to-rule' - but that's another story!'

Since the previous contributor has had the temerity to mention the Padre it is appropriate for us to seek a view of the proceedings from the alternative camp, so to speak. Padre Schofield was well known and has put pen to paper:

'I had two postings to Locking, the first in 1953. I was to report on 1 April and arrived to find there was a stand-down. New to the Service I was not impressed by its efficiency! I was given a temporary ID card and, a week or so later, I returned from a visit home to find an exercise in progress. The Station was to be invaded and invaders would be known by their forged ID cards! Arrested, I was frogmarched to the CO and, en route, saw one of the few officers I'd come to know. 'There's someone who knows me', I said. 'Never seen you in my life' he replied. The CO sent me to the guardroom for interrogation - their first prisoner. I could see they were going to enjoy the grilling they would give me when there was commotion outside, flour thrown on the guardroom wall, and we were told there had been a direct hit. The stupid nits were continuing to question me when I said, 'pack it in - we've all had it! It's my turn to question you now! What's the state of your eternal soul?' We laughed, I suggested we got out the cards, and we finished the exercise playing gin rummy!

The officer who 'didn't know me' became a great pal and gave me a big laugh! He had taken his car into Weston for servicing and had been wearing his uniform. Just missing a return bus, and knowing he had a quarter of an our to wait, he popped into the gents. In the next stall to him was a young apprentice who, seeing a uniformed officer beside him, immediately swung around with a smart salute and an equally smart 'Sir!'. Unfortunately he was still pee-ing and my pal's uniform was soaked! Coming into the Mess later, laughing and with trousers still sopping wet, he said, 'don't know whether to put him on a charge, and if I do what do I put on the charge sheet?'

Padre's Hours were always a challenge, but not without their humour. One lad asked about the miracle stories and particularly the feeding of the 5,000. He was broad Lancashire and said, 'feeding thousands o'folk with just a few loaves an' fishes - it's just daft!' A cockney apprentice immediately responded with,

'Blimey, padre, yer don't wanna bother abaht that - the RAF cooks are doin' it every day!'. One lad was particularly quick-witted and always good for a laugh - usually at my expense. He had a thing about free love - advocated it on every possible occasion - any time, any place, anyone! Then he fell in love. A lovely girl. Soon afterwards I went into Padre's Hour and said, 'Look chaps, I wonder if you'll help me out. You're the senior entry and I wondered if you'd take over running the Club tonight. I can't be there - but for God's sake don't tell my wife. I've got a date, and boy, oh boy am I going to have a whale of a time. Don't know whether she's easy, but by God I'll try! I'm going out with ....' and I mentioned the girlfriend's name. Quick as a flash he responded with, 'You're bloody well not!' 'Why not?' I asked. 'If it's OK for you - then why not for me?' The lads were on my side and the point was made.

Occasionally Padre's Hours started early 0815. I got up one dark morning, crept quietly around the house so as not to disturb my wife and, during the Padre's Hours, reached into a pocket for a handkerchief only to pull out a pair of my wife's knickers which I'd accidentally picked up. It took a long time to live that one down!

Harold was a cinema projectionist who helped out occasionally when we showed films in Padre's Hours. Although he professed to be an atheist he began to come along to the Club room and helped in a wide variety of ways. He volunteered to help in Sunday School but my wife pointed out to him that this would be difficult for an atheist. Nevertheless she asked him to give a general helping hand without any direct commitment, and certainly no teaching of the children. On posting we lost contact for a while but eventually I had a message of greeting sent through the Padre in Aden. There had been exceptionally heavy rain and, with inadequate drainage, the church was flooded. It was a Saturday and the Padre was mopping up in preparation for Sunday when two airmen volunteered to help. One was Harold. Again he professed to be an atheist, asked if the Padre knew me, and sent his greetings. Time passed. When stationed at RAF Coltishall I arranged for a young WAAF corporal to attend a Moral Leadership Course for lay preachers and she brought back photographs of herself and others on the course. Yes, you've guessed it… Harold was there. He was soon to leave the RAF and begin his training to become a Methodist Minister. When I expressed surprise the corporal said, 'Gosh, it must have been you he talked about - and Mrs 'S', and how she used to wash his socks because he had sweaty feet.' I'd forgotten that but mention of it brought a nostalgic pong to my nostrils!

Praise

We had a small group of apprentices who met each week with a young flight lieutenant to prepare for services which they took in local village churches. They did a fantastic job, were exceptionally good, and sometimes took services for me when I was away. After one such service, I heard nothing but praise from some who had been there. 'Brilliant!', one lad said, 'Far better than we usually have!'… a smack in the eye for me! I was concerned to know what was different and was told that the lad who took the service stood out in front before the service began and said, 'Look you lot, I'm usually there with you and I'm always disgusted with the way you talk during the collection. That's just as much part of the service as anything else. I know you won't stop it so we're going to take the collection now. The service hasn't started so you can natter as much as you bloody well like.' The collection was taken, everyone laughed and talked, the collection was brought forward for dedication and he said, 'Right, that's it, you've had your natter and the service is going to begin so for God's sake - and I mean that, for God's sake - shut up!' The service then

The Old Church

Apprentice memories

proceeded as usual but he'd grabbed their attention. It was different.

I was chaplain at Locking for the opening of the first purpose-built church in the UK. Prior to this we had always used huts.

It was a time of close cooperation between the three churches and the chaplains, but the Roman Catholics were still forbidden to join in worship with other denominations. The RC chaplain had been particularly helpful and I would dearly have loved him to take some part in the service. A higher power decreed that this could not be. The solution? At his suggestion my folk were relieved of all responsibility for arranging the social gathering which followed the service and so were free to attend the service after which we all went over to the RC clubroom for slap-up refreshments. Happily there came a time when we were all able to join in worship together. I remember well the first time this happened - it was a Battle of Britain service and my C of E colleague and I agreed to ask the RC chaplain to preach. He did. It is a sermon I shall never forget both for its content and its brevity. I give it to you in detail! In his broad Scottish accent he said, 'Ye all know why we're here - we're here to give thanks to God and to give thanks to the few. Thanks! Amen!' That was it! Much appreciated, I must say, by the apprentices, many of whom I know have remembered it.

The dedication service itself was not without incident. The CO is no longer with us so this story can now be told. He read the lesson beautifully - clear, distinct, and with an awareness of the occasion. No doubt it was nerves which made him read not the testimonies of Solomon but the testicles of Solomon! Only one apprentice showed signs of giggling, but he was frozen into silence by my wife's icy glance! There was a tape of the service and the following morning one of the technicians came into my office to say that they'd cut out the old man's testicles and, at almost the same moment, my organist came rushing in to say that 'the old man's testicles are all over the station!' Later that day the CO called me into his office. Thanking me for all I had done it was obvious that he had something else to say. 'Can't understand it, Padre. I knew that passage almost word for word but, just at the moment, I glanced down at the reading - and the testicles just slipped out. What I can't understand is that I never call them that!'

My second tour of duty at Locking was because the elderly chaplain serving there found padre's hour too much, was due to retire, and requested a final overseas tour. To accommodate him I was short-toured in Singapore and not at all happy about it. Maybe he was the chaplain of whom a lovely story is told. As is customary an officer on posting is dined-out of the Mess. Customarily he will make a farewell speech saying how much he has enjoyed his tour and how, though looking forward to his next job, he will miss his old station. Not this padre! He'd hated it and, to his credit, he was an honest man. His farewell speech might be summarised, 'You know I've not been happy here, and I've one regret. As I arrived on posting to the Station I was given some advice and I didn't take it. There, facing me in the road was a sign. It said 'Stop cock' and I didn't.'

> 'The old man's testicles were all over the Station.'

How many, I wonder, remember the tragic accident just down the Locking Road towards the airport? A dark night, car broken down, driver left his mate at the car while he walked back a little distance to the garage. A total electrics failure so no lights. Motorcycle ran into the car, pillion passenger bounced on top then into the road. Another car raced down, hit and carried the lad on the road about 50 yards before dropping him but didn't stop. The next day all car owners had to take their cars to the square where they were examined by the police. So far as I know no-one was ever caught.

Time and again I have told this story for a very specific reason. Between the accident and our assembling on the square there had been less than 24 hours yet already I had heard about a dozen different accounts of what happened. Interesting, I thought, that there are several accounts of the resurrection, and this - it had been argued many times in Padre's Hours - suggested that the story wasn't true. But, despite the different account of the accident, the basic fact was - someone had been killed. The central issue was undisputed and, indeed the fact was substantiated more

Apprentice memories

strongly by what seemed to be conflicting accounts.

There's always one among the officers - if you know what I mean. Flt Lt Smith (a false name) had a penchant for discipline and demanded a smart salute from any apprentice who came within sight of him. I remember between 20 and 30 lads arranging to walk towards him with a distance of some 15 to 20 yards between them. Each saluted smartly and each salute had to be returned. He never realised that after passing him they did a quick return to the back of the line and it must have seemed endless!

Some apprentices and others will remember that my hobby is ventriloquism and magic - great fun - and I cashed in on Flt Lt Smith's penchant for saluting by turning up for one of our many variety shows with my vent figure, Jimmie, having his arm in a sling. 'Kept bumping into that b**** Flight Lieutenant!' was all he needed to say and the audience convulsed with laughter.

Other officers, too, were gullible. I called one day on the CO when he and his wife were preparing for a party that evening. I gave a hand when suddenly his wife said, 'Oh, no! We're out of Remy Martin and you know what that... she hesitated... that so and-so is like'. She was referring to a certain Wing Commander who prided himself on his gastronomical finesse. He would savour the brandy, swirl it around in his glass, smell it, take a sip, and comment on its fine quality. With a wink the CO took a bottle of cheap NAAFI brandy, poured some in the Remy Martin bottle, and said, 'Let's see!' We did. Both the CO's wife and I had to escape to the kitchen in a fit of giggles as the Wing Commander went through his usual routine. I'll never know how the CO managed to control himself, but maybe that's the quality that singled him out for high office!

I recall the night when the CO shopped me! I had been invited to entertain at a charity function in Cheddar and was told that, because of family connections, a local vicar would also be attending - perhaps we could travel together? He would meet me on the road outside the Officers' Married Quarters. It was a very dark night, and carrying my quite large suitcase, I walked along the top road towards his car. Another car passed and, unknown to me, it was the CO. He didn't recognise me in the dark, assumed I could be a burglar getting away with the loot, and then saw the 'getaway' car and a dark-suited scarf-muffled stranger standing by. Without hesitation the CO made for the guardroom and by the time I arrived at the main road the local vicar was surrounded by 'snowdrops' who, until I arrived, would not believe his story!

The old church was a horse-shoe shaped building and had been a WAAF dining room. The closed end was the kitchen and store room and the two 'legs' were, on one side the church, on the other the clubroom. A helpful officer decided it would be much improved if, on the church side, we had a small belfry and bell. The belfry was erected without too much trouble, and the bell was installed. With great solemnity, but a lot of giggles, the officer rang the bell on the first Sunday after it was installed and we had the biggest rush to church one could imagine. He'd installed a fire bell not informed the guardroom, and in minutes the fire engine was there to put out the flames.

Not all was simple and straightforward, and some apprentices created problems. Girls from married quarters came along to the clubroom and I was approached by a SNCO because his daughter had been having nightmares - the obvious concern - a possible pregnancy, but no. Unknown to me one of the apprentices had begun to dabble in black magic, and he had obtained a key to get in and use the storeroom in the church. My first suspicion that something was wrong was when I discovered some candle wax on the plate used for Holy Communion. Then things were not quite in the places where I had left them. It transpired that, in order to placate - or to ward off- the evil spirits he had used the sacramental chalice and plate, together with the cross from the Communion Table, but this had in no way overcome the terrifying experiences which some who attended his session suffered. It was, you can well imagine, a traumatic time and confronted us with the possible closure of our clubroom indefinitely. Happily, because of my powers of persuasion, this did not happen. It made me realise, however - as if I did not know already - that apprentices are not little angels!'

Rescues
(as reported by the Weston Mercury)

Drama off Weston Beach

On 10 May 1962 two Apprentices swam half a mile to shore at Weston-super-Mare after their canoe had been capsized by rough seas. Weston lifeboatmen were called when the two were seen to be in difficulties off Brean Down. But with the tide behind them and two colleagues in another canoe alongside, the apprentices were able to reach the shore. Six apprentices were taking part in an initiative exercise, but had to turn back because of high seas. It was then that the one of the canoes capsized. From Birnbeck Island the lifeboatmen watched the drama unfold as finally the youths waded ashore, in the end the lifeboat was not needed.

Apprentices wade ashore

Apprentices save two lives on Bigbury Sands

In a separate incident on Bigbury Sands two apprentices, Richard Sharp and Terry Still, received gallantry awards for their part in a rescue of a 14 year old girl and her father. The apprentices were on summer camp at Collaton Cross and were sunbathing on the beach. The girl had drifted out to sea on an air bed and got into difficulty when she tried to swim back to the beach. Her father seeing her plight immediately went to her aid and also got into difficulty. Sharp and Still, who are both 18, had, with other apprentices been forbidden to swim because of the dangerous state of the seas. However, the two immediately entered the water and swam out to father and daughter bringing them to shore with the help of other apprentices who had taken an RAF boat out. On arrival at the shore the father was unconscious and Still applied artificial respiration. Both father and daughter recovered quickly from their ordeal after medical treatment.

The Royal Humane Society Award to Terry Still and Richard Sharp

Youths lost for 12 hours in Mendip Cave

Five aircraft apprentices of the 70th Entry were rescued on 2 May 1953 by members of the Bristol University Speleological Society after being lost for 12 hours in Read's Cavern. At 11pm on the Saturday when they had failed to return to camp, a road search was made by the RAF and civilian police. Another apprentice was able to tell the police that the five had gone to explore Read's Cavern. The police got in touch with the Bristol University team who were exploring in the area and by 1.45 am Sunday a five man team were on site to mount a rescue. The rescue party descended into the cave and found the five apprentices huddled in a water chamber at the bottom of the complex; fortunately they had the presence of mind to stay where they were after getting lost. It was 3.12am before the apprentices returned to Burrington Combe and were later released back to camp after being examined by a Doctor and found to be no worse for their experience.

88   Over and Out

Hamish with the Pipe Major

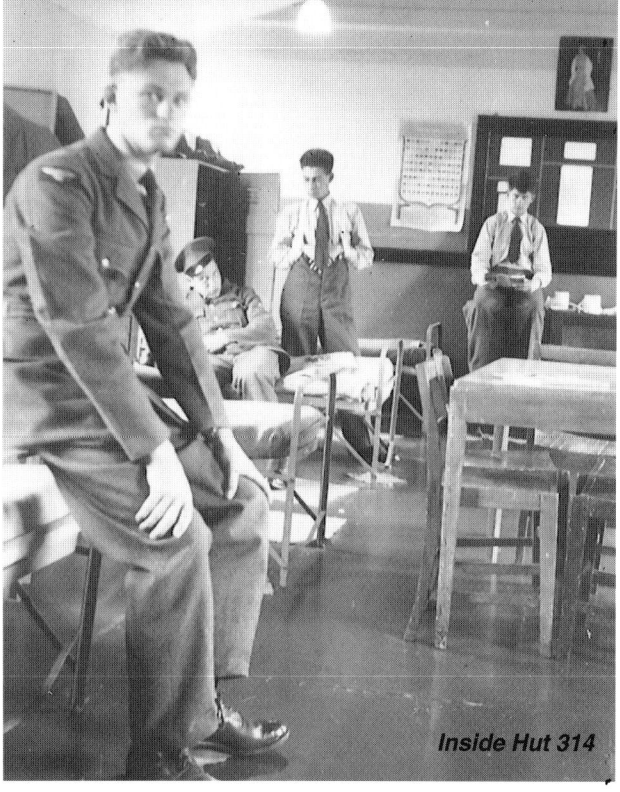

Inside Hut 314

Dougie Reid, now working for the Defence Housing Executive, was an apprentice from 1957-1960 and was also, as WO DJ Reid, the Adjutant of No 1 Radio School:

'In my apprentice days RAF Locking consisted of a large hutted camp. My first impressions were of a dank and dismal place, permanently wet and windy. We were accommodated in wooden billets sleeping some 22 men, each with his own area of brown polished lino.

Every morning started with laying out a blanket pack, leaving the billet ready for inspection with the brown floor polished to such a degree that everything reflected in it. We were not allowed to walk on the floor in those days and had to shuffle around with small pieces of blanket under the feet.

The whole of Apprentice Wing, numbering close to 1,000, would parade on the road around the apprentice accommodation by the sports field. After being inspected, the Wing would then march off to work led by the pipe band. Every Saturday morning there was a full parade, just like the Queen's Birthday Parade, on square with the Apprentice Wing and Wings of the regular and National Service trainees, accompanied by the Regional Band and the Apprentice Pipe and Fife Band.

With the exception of the last Sunday in the month, every Sunday was a full blown Church Parade marching to the church in the 3(T) Theatre.'

Winter on the Parade Square

Over and Out 89

The Western Band of the Royal Air Force

50 years of music 1947 - 1997

Compiled by Flt Lt GJ Bain - October 1997

Originally under the name of No. 5 Regional Band, the Western Band has been located at Royal Air Force Locking since early 1949 and has been, since then, an important feature of the Station. As a lodger unit controlled by Headquarters Music Services at Uxbridge, much of the Band's work has always been away from base. However, when apprentice training was at its peak, the Band played an integral part in Station life, providing music for the regular apprentice parades at a time when drilling and parading were used as a means to instil discipline and a sense of corporate pride in young airmen.

These days, however, on-Station appearances are a much rarer occurrence, and the Western Band's role now focuses more on maintaining and fostering the very good relationship RAF Locking enjoys with the surrounding community.

The following traces the development of the Western Band from the early days to the present through narrative, photographs and contributions from ex-Band members.

After the war, the Command Bands were re-established to form Regional Bands numbered one to six. All the bands, including the Regiment Band and the Central Band, were to come under the control of an Organising Director of Music at RAF Uxbridge. No. 5 Regional Band was formed at Bridgnorth in 1947 under the direction of Bandmaster HJL Cash, but was soon thereafter moved to Fighter Command at Stanmore and then on to Buckeburg in occupied Germany.

This 25 piece band remained in Germany until early 1949 travelling widely in the British Occupied Zone, but never as far as Berlin. On the very Sunday morning the Band was due to fly from Gutersloh to Berlin to entertain the Russians, the Berlin Blockade began and the job was cancelled.

In January 1949, and, by all accounts, much to the relief of the musicians, No. 5 Regional Band returned to the UK to be located at RAF

No. 5 Regional Band in Hamburg, 1947

90 Over and Out

The Western Band of the RAF

Transport problems in Bristol, 1955.

Locking where it was given a somewhat cool reception by the Station Commander. Dougie Arthur recounts:

'When we got there, the CO approached Bandmaster Cash and said, 'I don't want your musicians sleeping on my camp. I'm not having all your unsocial hours, coming in at one, two in the morning. I want you all to live in town. So tell your boys to go out and get themselves digs.' The living out allowance was £1 35d a week, and I went to the West End Hotel in Weston-super Mare.'

This Station policy, which allowed musicians to draw their ration money and live out, was, apparently, unique to RAF Locking and stayed in place until the new Bandroom was built at the north-west end of the camp in 1969 when the adjacent Nicholson Block became the Band accommodation.

Contrasting

In the days of National Service, life in the RAF was characterized by contrasting people from a wide variety of backgrounds. This was no more evident than in the bands since topflight professional musicians would, naturally, try to opt for service as a musician when called up. This factor increased the already wide variation in playing standards within the bands, as John Foley recalls:

'We had this wonderful oboist with the Band, Roger Winfield. Roger came to the Band from the Halle Orchestra. Anyway, the Bandmaster said, 'Now listen boys, we've got this guy coming and he's from the Halle! So what we'll do, don't worry, we'll make it look good. Every morning the Silken Ladder, Rossini.' So we rehearsed the Silken Ladder inside out, upside down and backwards until we could play it beautifully. So this day, Roger turned up and the Bandmaster said, 'Oh, hello Roger, would you like to sit down. This is Roger Winfield, chaps. I think this morning we'll play.... the Silken Ladder.' So off we went and, of course, he was a brilliant player. Well, gradually the Band lost their place and gradually it went quieter and quieter until, in the end, there was only him playing. Then, when he'd finished, we all clapped.'

The expansion of the RAF Music Services and the creation of a network of Regional Bands led, in the early 1950s, to a shortfall of qualified bandmasters and directors of music that had implications for No. 5 Regional Band in late 1953, as Henry Hall explains:

'Flt Lt Lambourne passed away with Leukaemia. Well, they'd run out of bandmasters and we'd got a reputation. The voluntary bandmaster came down from Stanmore and he was with us a very short time, and then he slipped a disc. So we were disbanded and I went to Henlow.'

Shortage

No. 5 Regional Band was re-established in 1954 under Fg Off Vic Hutchinson who had been attracted into the RAF from the Royal Marines by the opportunities for rapid promotion presented by the shortage of qualified bandmasters. This was to be the first of three tours as Director of Music at RAF Locking for Vic Hutchinson who had joined the Royal Marines as a band boy in 1936, serving on the cruiser, *HMS Neptune*, and the battleship, *HMS Warspite*, during World War Two. Since leaving the Service in 1976, Sqn

The Western Band of the RAF

Pass-Out Parade in 1956. The photograph shows Post Office Road in the background.

Ldr Hutchinson has remained a prominent member of the Officers' Mess, conspicuous by his chest-full of campaign medals collected during a long Service career.

Originally, No. 5 Regional Band's Bandroom was located off the corner of the parade square, close to where the Medical Centre is now. This wooden hut was heated by a stove in the centre of the rehearsal room and surrounded by a high wall built, allegedly, to protect the rest of the Station from the Band. In 1961, the Band moved to occupy three huts on Post Office Road with the rehearsal room in one hut and the music library and stores in another. The third was a dormitory hut used as holding accommodation for newly posted-in musicians searching for digs in town. The threat of being made to live in this accommodation was also found to be a useful means of deterring the single living-out airmen from minor acts of indiscipline.

Throughout the 1950s and 1960s, the working schedule of the Band was stabilized to a certain extent by the regular routine of parades and rehearsals taking place at RAF Locking itself. Once a month there was a 'CO's Parade' which involved all the apprentices. They were marched on by their own pipe and

The Band marches past on the first occasion of RAF Locking exercising the Freedom of Weston-super-Mare in 1956.

92   Over and Out

The Western Band of the RAF

The Western Band competing for the Sims Cup Trophy on RAF Locking's Parade Square in 1976.

drum band while the permanent staff were marched on by No. 5 Regional Band, which also performed the inspection pieces. There were also the pass out parades for the apprentice courses coming up at regular intervals and, taken together, these parades would constitute a large chunk of the Band's monthly routine.

Involvement of the Band on Station would decrease as the apprentice courses began to move away; whereas substantial cuts in the number of established RAF bands over a 15 year period between 1964 and 1979 would see the Band travelling ever farther and wider.

In 1964, the Near East Air Force Band, based in Cyprus, was disbanded and thereafter No. 5 Regional Band was issued with 'Whites' and allocated an annual summer tour of the Middle East calling at Cyprus, Malta, Gibraltar and the Persian Gulf bases of Sharjar, Masirah and Salalah.

Otherwise, the Band's schedule consisted mainly of parade work at RAF stations in Wales and the South-West Region and, although this didn't involve great distances by today's standards, it still meant a lot of time on the road with plenty of overnight stops, as Sam Hansford explains:

The Western Band being inspected by Her Majesty, The Queen, at RAF Locking in 1986.

Over and Out   93

The Western Band of the RAF

'One regular trip was to St Athan in South Wales and, of course, you have to remember that there were no bridges then, there were no motorways. So to go to St Athan was about an eight or nine hour journey. So you had to go right the way up around Gloucester, come down the other side of the Severn Estuary and go right the way down to St Athan. And that would be an overnight stop.'

There were three major developments that characterized the late 1960's and early 1970's period. The first was in 1968, when the then Organising Director of Music, Wg Cdr JL Wallace, decided to dispense with the system of numbering the regional bands, a system which he had always considered suggested a pecking order. He gave the bands proper names and from 1 January 1969, No. 5 Regional Band became known as the Western Band of the Royal Air Force.

The second development was the move to the new Bandroom in 1969, and the third was the disbandment of the Far East Air Force Band in November 1970. The long-term effect of this was to allow for a more permanent nucleus of personnel to develop within the Western Band, as the existence of the Far and Near East Bands had always generated a high level of posting turnover with in the UK bands.

In 1977, as part of a round of defence cuts, the Southern Band of the Royal Air Force, formerly known as No. 4 Regional Band, was disbanded. This meant that the Western Band was the only one of the six original regional bands remaining. Not that the regional title had great significance any more, as the development of the motorway network had now made it possible to task the Western Band to most places in the UK with ease.

The mid 1970s saw the last apprentice courses move away from RAF Locking, and thereafter the Western Band's involvement on Station settled to an annual routine that included the Freedom Parade, the Battle of Britain Reception and Sunset Ceremony, the Flowerdown Fair, a Christmas Concert for the local senior citizens and appearances for guest nights in the Officers' Mess.

Otherwise, the Band would appear for Station concerts at the Playhouse Theatre in Weston-super-Mare, and play for a wider audience of senior citizens at the Winter Gardens at Christmas Time. The Band would also perform at local care institutions such as the William Knowles Centre and Bay Tree Special Needs School as well as at other schools in the area.

This routine was rudely interrupted during

Musicians of the Western Band in Kuwait after the Gulf War.

The Western Band of the RAF

The Western Band at the RAF Akrotiri Open Day in 1996.

the Gulf Crisis of 1990-91, however, when the musicians of the Western Band deployed to Saudi Arabia as medical orderlies. At the time a newly commissioned Flying Officer and Director of Music, Duncan Stubbs, recalls the day war broke out for the Western Band:

'When we got the news we were at Aldergrove, fog bound, couldn't get back, and I took a phone call in the Mess behind the servery and it was Rob Wiffin on the phone. He said, 'have you got your pen and paper?' and I could tell straight away from the tone of his voice that something was wrong. Anyway, he gave me these dates: '7 - 14 December, you're going to Satan Camp, and then you're off to the Gulf.' On arrival in Saudi Arabia, the Band was divided into two with half going to Al Qaysumah on the front line with No. 1 Aero-Medical Evacuation Squadron (AES), and the remainder staying with 4626 AES at Al Jubayl further to the south.

The members of the Western Band acquitted themselves admirably during the Gulf War, demonstrating that musicians are usually intelligent and adaptable people, capable of being an asset to the Service in any situation. Today, the Western Band is in demand for its musical excellence, representing the Royal Air Force locally, nationally and internationally.

In 1996, for example, the Band performed in the Falkland Islands, Ascension Island, Germany, Cyprus as well as accompanying Her Majesty, The Queen, on a State Visit to Thailand. This in addition to two trips to Northern Ireland, a visit to the Isle of Man and many other routine engagements besides.

With the closure of RAF Locking in 1999, the relocation of the Western Band is inevitable. With that, the name will disappear forever, and this is just one example of the many ways in which the histories of RAF Locking and the Western Band are inextricably linked.

Over the past 50 years, both parties have enjoyed an association of which all can justifiably be proud, and, although the Station closure will mark the end of an era for many RAF musicians, the foregoing demonstrates how strongly the memories will remain.

The Western Band of the RAF

Western Band of the Royal Air Force

Directors of music

Flt Lt HJL Cash MBE RAF	1949-1951
Flt Lt F Lambourne MBE RAF	1951-1954
Fg Off V Hutchinson LRAM ARCM RAF	1954-1957
Fg Off JE Wagner RAF - 1958-1958	
Flt Lt R Ponsford LRAM ARCM RAF	1959-1960
Fg Off D G Robinson FTCL LRAM ARCM ARCO(ChM) RAF	1960
Flt Lt J Martindale LRAM ARCM RAF	1960-1964
Sqn Ldr V Hutchinson LRAM ARCM RAF	1964-1966
Sqn Ldr R Ponsford LRAM ARCM RAF	1966-1967
Sqn Ldr J Martindale LRAM ARCM RAF	1967-1971
Sqn Ldr V Hutchinson LRAM ARCM RAF	1971-1976
Sqn Ldr DS Stephens LRAM ARCM RAF	1976-1977
Flt Lt I Kendrick LRAM ARCM RAF	1978-1983
Flt Lt F Ashford FTCL LRAM ARCM RAF	1983-1985
Flt Lt RK Wiffin BA FTCL LRAM ARCM RAF	1985-1990
Flt Lt DJG Stubbs BA(Hons) ARCM LGSM ANCM RAF	1990 - 1995
Flt Lt GJ Bain BA LRAM ARCM M1L RAF	1995-

96 Over and Out

Royal Air Force Amateur Radio Society

In October 1996, although the future of RAF Locking was then still uncertain, it was decided to move the RAFARS headquarters and 'Voice of the Air' from RAF Locking to RAF Cosford. The handover occurred on 1 October, exactly 45 years to the day after the Society's headquarters moved from RAF Cranwell. At a ceremony on the air using callsign GX8FC, as the Society's Vice President, the Station Commander handed over the 'Voice of the Air' to the RAF Cosford Amateur Radio Club, via their Station Commander. The Society's Vice Presidency and administration would remain at RAF Locking for the time being. Of particular note is that 1996 was also the Diamond Jubilee of the formation of the Cranwell Amateur Radio Transmitting Society, the forerunner of RAFARS.

The RAFARS hut at RAF Locking underwent a major re-equipment in September 1962, as reported by the *Weston Mercury*:

The hut then contained the most modern equipment available which was capable of worldwide communications on the amateur bands, the main transmitter being the only one of its type in the country. All of the new equipment is American as there was, at the time, no comparable British equipment available. A new system of aerials was also constructed which included a 360ft horizontal aerial and a beam aerial. Of the £800 total cost, £660 had been granted by the Nuffield Trust, the remainder coming from within the Society. Collins Radio Equipment as the supplier installed the equipment free of charge. RAFARS already held the call sign GX8FC but on handover were also licensed to use G3RAF.

To coincide with the re-equipment programme a regional rally of the Radio Society of Great Britain was held on the Beach Lawns where one of the official guests was AVM CM Stewart - Director General of Signals. The rally included what has been described as 'Weston's First Mobile Radio Rally' where competitors would have to navigate around a pre-determined route and maintain radio contact with three radio stations.

RAFARS was rather taken by surprise by the news of the launch of an artificial satellite by the Russians on 3 November 1957. This surprise, shared by the rest of the world, was increased when it was found out that the satellite was radiating at a frequency of 20MHz and 40MHz when by international agreement it was supposed to be radiating at 108MHz. This lead to some

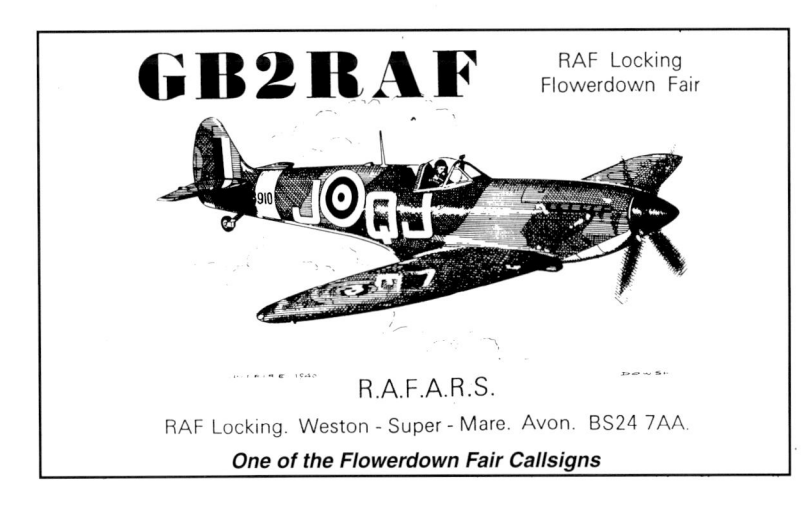

RAFARS Headquarters in 1962

GB2RAF — RAF Locking Flowerdown Fair

R.A.F.A.R.S.
RAF Locking. Weston - Super - Mare. Avon. BS24 7AA.
One of the Flowerdown Fair Callsigns

Over and Out 97

consternation since RAFARs had been prepared to monitor the agreed frequency. The news led to hurried preparations and within two and a half hours sufficient equipment was cobbled together to allow monitoring to begin. More was added in the next 48 hours and by the fourth day observers were satisfied with the accuracy of the method and its reliability.

The observations occupied approximately 17 minutes of each orbit when readings of audio frequency output against time were taken. These were converted into graphs and sent to the central coordinating agency at Norwood Technical College. The observers at RAF Locking were visited by the Press on many occasions and the success of their achievement can be judged by the fact that they continued their observation for seven days at the request of the Cavendish Laboratory at Cambridge, this period being well beyond the usual 48 hours expected from most amateur observers.

The RAF Locking Radio Society, part of RAFARS, has always displayed at Flowerdown Fair for the benefit of visitors and members and a log is kept of the day's contacts.

Connections with the Royal Family

Since the Station was opened in 1939 there have been many Royal Visitors to the Station and, in addition, personnel have always played a full part in celebrating and supporting events associated with Royal Patronage.

In July 1940 His Royal Highness, Gp Capt The Duke of Kent visited the Station and this was repeated the following year in April 1941 when the Station was graced by a return visit by His Royal Highness Air Cdre The Duke of Kent.

On 15 August 1950 a ceremonial parade was held to mark the occasion of the birth of a daughter to Her Royal Highness Princess Elizabeth.

A King's Birthday Parade was held on 7 June 1951 and a Royal Standard was paraded at RAF Locking for the first time.

Her Royal Highness Princess Margaret visited the Station on 23 May 1953 as part of her tour of Somerset Youth Organisations. Aircraft Apprentices formed a Guard of Honour and were praised for their smartness, excellent bearing and turnout. The day was hot and all the vehicles were in open top order and the Land Rovers had all been resprayed white for the occasion.

In the morning before Her Royal Highness arrived it was discovered that, although the Land Rovers had been resprayed, the paint job did not extend under the canvas tilt so that when the tilt was removed the khaki green support structure was revealed. This was hurriedly painted but unfortunately the paint would not be dry for the visit, but no one would notice would they? The officer who had to

HRH Princess Margaret arrives at RAF Locking

stand in the back on the Land Rover to escort HRH did notice because as soon as the Land Rover moved off he caught hold of the newly painted cross bar with both brown gloved hands to steady himself. Throughout the day, unknown to him, he exchanged salutes with a brown glove decorated by white 'invasion stripes'!

On 26 July 1955 Her Royal Highness Princess Margaret reviewed the 72 Entry Aircraft Apprentices on the occasion of their Passing Out Parade.

Royal Connections

The 83 Entry Aircraft Apprentices were reviewed at their Passing Out Parade by Her Royal Highness Princess of Gloucester on 24 March 1959.

Over the years numerous apprentices and trainees have taken part in the Duke of Edinburgh's Award Scheme and, in 1965, 14 received personnel invitations to attend Gold Award Presentation Ceremonies at Buckingham Palace. Each of these ceremonies on 11 May, 8 July and 23 November was presided over by the Duke of Edinburgh himself.

HRH Princess Margaret meets Hamish and the 72nd Entry

HRH Princess of Gloucester with Group Captain Chamberlain

Sixty eight apprentices lined the route for the wedding of Her Royal Highness Princes Anne and Captain Mark Phillips on 14 November 1973.

Her Royal Highness Princess Margaret Countess of Snowden visited the Station on 25 June 1974 when she saw many aspects of the training and recreational facilities. The bells of Locking Village church concluded the day by peeling out 'Westminster' in honour of Her Royal Highness's visit.

HRH Princess of Gloucester with Gp Capt Holroyd

Over and Out 99

Royal Connections

Signing the Visitor's Book in the Officers' Mess

Meeting the People

On 28 May 1978 Her Royal Highness Princess Anne as Patron of St John's Ambulance attended a Cadet Rally held at RAF Locking during which 1,400 cadets and 300 officers were paraded and reviewed by Her Royal Highness.

Air Marshal Her Royal Highness Princess Alice, Duchess of Gloucester visited the Station on 23 May 1979 and was pleased to meet a wide cross section of personnel engaged in training, welfare and recreational activities.

Planning

Her Majesty The Queen visited RAF Locking on 30 October 1986 where she viewed the School's training facilities and met many of the Station's personnel and families. For this visit

HRH Princess Alice on a Tour of the Station

the Station had prepared for every eventuality, including the weather and meticulous planning had gone into planning for both outdoor and indoor parades. On the day, of course, it rained and plan 'B' sprung into action for a wet weather parade in 3 (T) Block. However, someone noticed a large umbrella stood just inside the entrance and asked whether it was to shelter Her Majesty for the short walk from the car to the entrance? 'No', came the reply, 'it's to keep Her Majesty dry inside the building because the roof leaks like a sieve.'

In 1982 after the wedding of Lady Diana to the Prince of Wales the Royal Wedding Gifts were exhibited at a number of

Her Majesty is greeted by Gp Capt Heyes

Royal Connections

locations, including Bristol. RAF Locking assisted at the exhibition and were thanked by their Royal Highnesses through their Lady in Waiting.

BUCKINGHAM PALACE
From Miss A. Beckwith-Smith

24th November, 1982

Dear Group Captain Lewis,

The Prince and Princess of Wales have asked me to write and thank you and all the volunteers from RAF Locking who helped so splendidly and willingly with the Exhibition of wedding presents and Her Royal Highness's wedding dress in Bristol.

Their Royal Highnesses realise what an important and vital undertaking organising a roster of volunteers is to the successful conduct of the Exhibition and very much appreciate the excellent help which was so kindly given. The Prince and Princess are extremely grateful.

Their Royal Highnesses ask me to pass on to you and all those involved their most sincere and warm thanks.
Yours sincerely,
Anne Beckwith-Smith
Lady-in-Waiting

Group Captain KG Lewis

A letter expressing thanks from the Prince and Princess of Wales

---

HRH receives a bouquet of flowers

On 15 March 1991 Her Royal Highness The Princess of Wales paid a low key visit to the Station to meet the people who had contributed to the Gulf Support Group and to meet servicemen from the Western Band who had served in the Gulf as medical orderlies and stretcher bearers, together with their wives and families.

HRH Princess of Wales signs the Visitor's Book

Royal Connections

HRH Princess Margaret escorted by Gp Capt Sloss

The latest royal visitor Her Royal Highness Princess Margaret Countess of Snowden visited the Station on 24 May 1994. The ORB records that 'despite the wet and blustery weather the full programme of events was completed. Her Royal Highness had expected to see more trainees than she did, and was somewhat surprised when it was explained how low the student numbers had fallen in the aftermath of the collapse of the Soviet Union.'

Aircraft at RAF Locking

Despite the 'waterfront' appearance of the training blocks and the closeness of Weston Airfield, RAF Locking has never been used for flying activities.

However, for many years RAF Locking trained aircraft mechanics and so it is not surprising that many aircraft, some notable, would end their days here as training vehicles.

In addition there have been a succession of 'Gate Guardians' of various types. The following is a list of those aircraft that are known about with some history.

The list does not claim to be exhaustive and much of this information has been provided by K Michael Yates who is an Aviation Research Historian:

VV 366 in Operational Livery

102 *Over and Out*

Gate Guardians

1970 - 1986	LA198	Spitfire XXI	
1962 - 1967	MK356	Spitfire LF IXC (Now being restored at St Athan)	
NK - 1966	XA564	Javelin FAW1	
1966 - NK	WL360	Meteor T7	Sold
1974 - NK	WH840	Canberra T4	Sold
1992- 1996	XM708	Gnat TMk 1	Sold

Aircraft used for training

5 Sof TT

1940 - 1941	K6155	Anson Mk 1	
1940 - NK	K6304	Anson Mk 1	
1940 - 1943	K8822	Anson Mk 1	
1946	DG202	Meteor F9/40	> Prototypes now on display at RAF Museum RAF Cosford
1946	DG207	Meteor F9/40	
1945	EE220	Meteor F1	
1945	EE225	Meteor F1 >	1st production batch
1946	EE228	Meteor F1	
1948	EE391	Meteor F3	
N/K	WT616	Hunter F1	

No 1 RS

1950 - 1957	W365	Anson T21	
1950 - 1951	W366	Anson T21	
1951	VV366	Anson T22	Sold
1961	XA919	Victor Mk 1	Prototype, flown in to Weston

The following article is extracted from the *Bristol Evening Post* and *Weston Mercury* of 22/23 November 1962:

'One of the few surviving Spitfires with record of wartime operations is to have a permanent home at RAF Locking. The Spitfire is a Mk IX - MK356 which will be mounted on a 'flying plinth' located near the Main Gate.

This machine joined 443 Squadron of the RCAF at RAF Digby in March 1944. This squadron was part of the 'Canadian Wing' led by Wg Cdr JE (Johnny) Johnson. During the week preceding the invasion of Europe the Wing operated from the South Coast on low level fighter strikes and escort duties and was flying from Normandy shortly after D Day. In August 1944 MK356 was relegated to a servicing unit and its operational career was ended.

After the war it was renumbered 5690M and transferred to RAF Halton for instructional use and in 1951 went to RAF Hawkinge for display until that station closed in 1961. With the passing of time and the addition of successive layers of silver paint the Spitfire's original identity was forgotten, until 1958 when some of the RAF Hawkinge personnel restored it to a more appropriate finish.

Now it has been refurbished over a period of eight months by a team of personnel from RAF Locking's station workshops.

All the external apertures have been resealed and it has been completely stripped and repainted in its wartime camouflage colours of disrupted brown and green on the upper surfaces and duck egg blue underneath. The workshop staff have also manufactured all the fittings to hold the aircraft on its plinth

MK 356 at the Main Gate

The finishing touches outside the Bellman Hangar

and constructed the shuttering for forming the concrete, the plinth itself being constructed by the Airfield Construction Branch. The Rolls Royce Merlin is still fitted in the airframe but there is no other equipment. The landing wheels have been removed and the undercarriage has been retracted."

(The Spitfire remained at RAF Locking until 1967 when it was removed into store. It has now resurfaced again at St Athan where it is being restored into flying condition with a first flight scheduled before the end of 1997).

WH 840, the Canberra T4, was delivered to RAF Bassingbourne, 231 OCU, in March 1954 and remained there until 1962, completing 2140 hrs as a flying trainer. After 231 OCU the aircraft continued its flying service at RAF Tangmere, RAF Watton and Boscombe Down before moving to Germany in 1966. From then until its retirement in 1970 it was used for Operational Techniques and Weapon Training. WH 840's last flight was to St Athan.

The Gnat, XM 708, entered service with

Being hoisted onto the plinth

CFS at RAF Little Rissington on 10 May 1962, moving to No 4 FTS at RAF Valley on the 31 st August 1972.

In its chequered career at No 4 FTS it received Cat 3 damage on no less than three occasions, each time being repaired at 14 MU before being returned to service - says something for the skills of trainee pilots and RAF technicians, they bend em we mend em! On 2 December 1977 XM 708 was finally retired with not much left of the original aircraft

In Operational Colours

and allocated for ground instructional duties at RAF Halton receiving the Maintenance Serial No 8573M. On arrival at RAF Locking it was decided to mount it in an attitude that was described as 'a split second away from a nasty prang' befitting its treatment in the hands of the 'winged few' at RAF Valley. Though resplendent in Red Arrows livery it was never actually flown by the team.

Aircraft tradesman gained experience on a wide variety of training aircraft in the Bellman Hangars, but in the late 1950's these were all transferred to a hangar at the far end of Weston airfield, it was thought to be more realistic to provide training in an airfield environment. To meet the need for modern aircraft a Victor MkI XA 919 was flown into Weston airfield. The date of the event was widely publicised and a large body of the local population turned out to watch the event, with some trepidation because there was not much runway to spare.

Spitfire F21 LA 198 flew with No 1 and No 602 squadrons during the war and on demote was sent to the 3rd Civil Anti-Aircraft Cooperation Unit. However, in 1954 it was transferred from RAF Cosford to Perdiswell in Worcester where it graced the ATC base until 1967 when it was recovered for use in the film Battle of Britain. Afterwards it did not return to Worcester but was moved to RAF Locking as a Gate Guardian. After this it moved to RAF Leuchars for a time and then into storage at Cardington. It has now, just recently, been released again by the MOD to finally lie in the City of Glasgow museum.

XM 708 at the Gate

The Great Rebuilding Plan

The Officers' Mess with Morris Oxford SPC 395 owned by Mrs Williams

Station Headquarters situated opposite the Main Gate

In the early 1960s there was the great redevelopment plan to replace the ageing wooden hutted accommodation with something more permanent and modern. Written in 1962 this article reproduced from the 'Locking Review' sets out the intention:

'It has long been intended to put into effect an extensive programme of rebuilding and modernisation at RAF Locking. Apart from the practical value and comfort of modern brick-built accommodation, many have felt that such a project would give a considerable boost to the morale of permanent staff and trainees alike, while, at the same time, creating in the minds of our many visitors a more pleasing and a more accurate impression of the high standards required and achieved.

As is obvious from the appearance of certain areas of the Station, this development project is now under way. This article is intended to explain the progress of the plan hitherto and to give an idea of what RAF Locking will look like when the rebuilding has

The Intended Site Plan

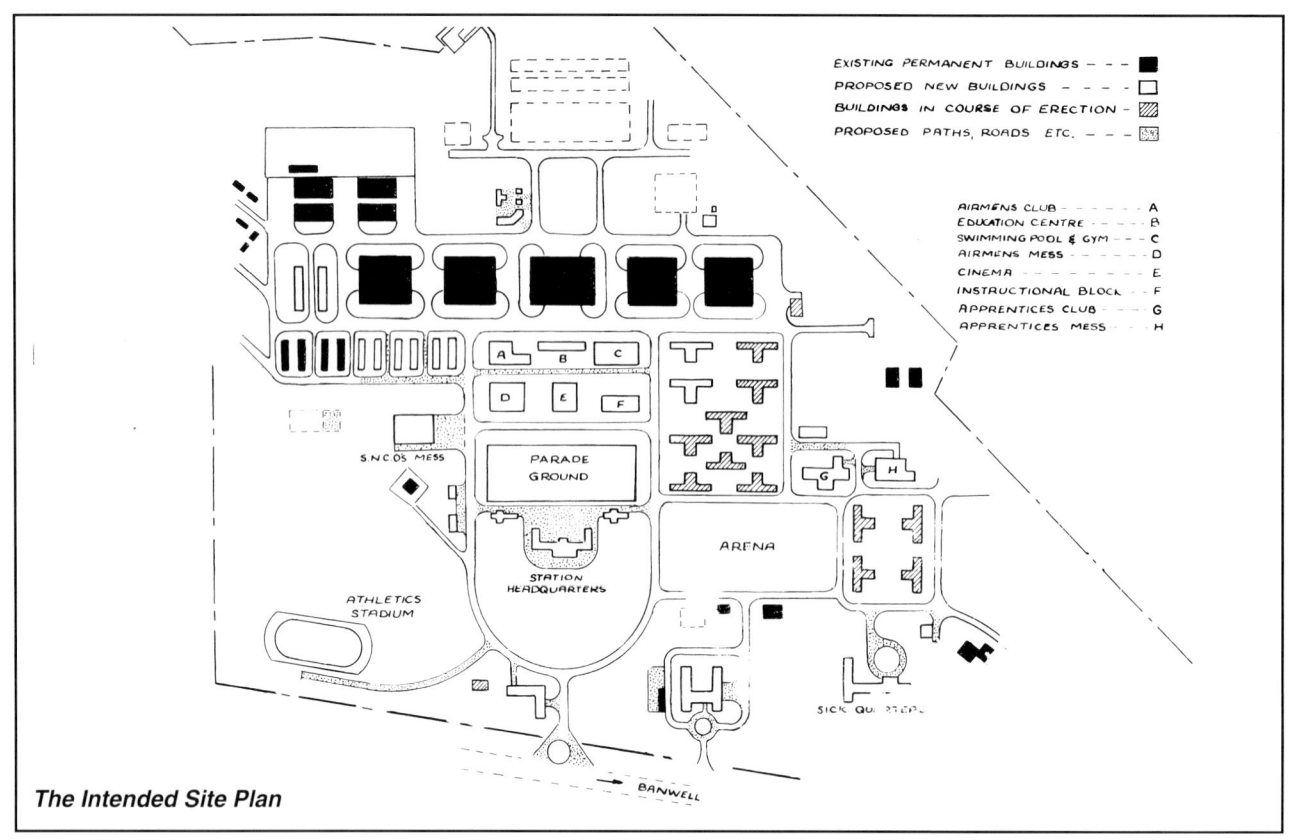

been completed.

The object is to demolish all wooden buildings and replace them with permanent, modern, brick buildings taking approximately five to six years to complete.

The first phase is to re-accommodate trainees and permanent staff in modern, centrally heated, comfortable buildings, and a start was made on the Aircraft Apprentice barrack blocks about 12 months ago.

Altogether plans were made for 14 apprentice barrack blocks, each block to accommodate 80 apprentices. At the time of writing four blocks have been completed and are occupied. Another eight blocks will have been completed before the end of this year.'

It was thought in 1968 that the barrack blocks should be named to be aesthetically pleasing and in choosing 'heroe's' names there would be a beneficial effect on morale. The intention was to name the 21 newly built airmen's and apprentices' barrack blocks after Victoria Cross holders of the Royal Flying Corps and the Royal Air Force:

Nicholson	Cheshire
Manser	Hannah
Garland	Mottershead
Cruikshank	Mannock
Thompson	Gray
Hawker	Aaron
Lord	Bishop
Ball	McCudden
Scarf	Jackson
Robinson	Gibson

The four training blocks were also to have

Barrack Blocks - Before and After

been given names, but of famous people associated with the world of electronics:

1(T) Marconi Block
2(T) Watson Watt Block
3(T) Faraday Block
4(T) Maxwell Block
5(T) Babbage Block

They will take approximately one year to build and if work is commenced, as expected, in September of this year, there is every hope that they will be opened towards the end of 1963. At the same time a new instructional block is to be built on the site occupied at present by 'A' Squadron, Apprentice Wing, Headquarters, while on the site at present used for overflow classrooms for apprentice training, five adult training blocks are to be built, each block to accommodate 80 airmen. As in the case of the Apprentice Mess and Club, these buildings will start in the early autumn of 1962 and should take approximately one year to build. At the completion of these projects, it is calculated that all permanent staff and trainees, both airmen and apprentices, will be in modern living accommodation.

The building of 5(T) Block

The new Apprentice Wing HQ - now demolished

St Andrew's PMUB Church

We also hope soon to commence the building of a new Anglican church, which will be built on the site of the present PMUB church. This is being replaced by a new PMUB church which can already be seen opposite the Education Section. The new PMUB church will soon be ready and the opening ceremony should take place sometime this summer.

The next phase will be the building of a new combined gymnasium and swimming pool which will be behind a new instruction block and directly opposite No. 2 (T) Block. At about the same time it is hoped that the new Sergeants' Mess will be built, and this is to be sited on the west side of McCrae Road and directly opposite Lower Parade Road. This project will be closely followed by a new Airmen's Mess, the 'Threepenny Bit', and Club, which is to be sited on the plot immediately to the west of the present No. 3 Area Mess and NAAFI. A new Station Sick Quarters, a new Adult Wing Headquarters and Apprentice Wing Headquarters are also projected at about the same time, the Sick Quarters being positioned on the site of the present Aircraft Apprentice NAAFI. By this time the new Apprentice Club will have been completed and no loss of tea and buns will be occasioned.

Next on the list is a new Officers' Mess, which is to be built on the same site as the existing Mess. While it is under construction the officers will take up residence in the present Sergeants' Mess, which by then will have been vacated. Station Headquarters is to be moved from its present site to one overlooking the southern boundary of the Station Parade Ground. The Anglican Church will be on the east side of the new headquarters as already explained, the Roman Catholic Church on the west side. An Education and Hobbies Centre will be constructed between the Airmen's Club and the swimming pool, directly opposite the present gymnasium. Behind this it is hoped to build a new Astra Cinema. Finally a new guardroom is to be built on the existing site and a new Families' Shop and Post Office will be constructed on the west side of McCrae Road, opposite the south-west corner of the Parade Ground.

It will be observed that a lot of excavation work has already commenced in the sports area of the south-west corner of the Station boundary. This is preliminary work to the construction of a full size sports stadium, giving all track and field event facilities, and in due course a No. 1 soccer pitch. In order to make this really worthwhile a PSI grandstand is to be built on the south side of the track from non-public funds. A grant of £5,000 was obtained from the Command Central Fund and the remainder is being provided from Service Institute Funds and by donations from the Officers' and Sergeants' Messes. The running track, being built by the Airfield Construction Branch, should be completed this summer and the grandstand by the end of the year, so that full benefit can be derived in next year's athletic season.

At the time of writing there are 155 airmen's married quarters and 61 officers' married quarters. In the near future contracts are to be let for the erection of a further 82 airmen's married quarters on the north-west corner of the camp, and a further 38 officers' married quarters.

So in five or six years' time, Locking will have had a complete face-lift. After the rubble and debris have been removed, the Station should present a very attractive and impressive countenance to the world. Certainly the amenities of Locking will be hard to equal at any home unit. In such an environment apprentices and airmen alike should find the incentive to live up to their surroundings and to add creditably to the record of RAF Locking.'

(As can now be seen the completed building programme did not quite match the planned and it is interesting to note with hindsight that the permanent concrete, steel and brick buildings have only proved marginally more durable than the wooden huts, indeed some of the 1960's buildings have been, or are scheduled to be, demolished).

Pictured left: Aerial view from Locking Village. Remnants of the old buildings remained for many years after the great re-build, notably the wooden medical centre was used for club activity until 1986 and the last Bellman Hangar was demolished in 1993.

'Let the Doors Be Opened'

(An account of the new church at RAF Locking)

The day of 6 September 1962 marked the opening and dedication of the new St Andrew's (PMUB) Church, which was the first permanent Church for 'other denominations' in the Royal Air Force to be built using public funds.

The church is modern, but does not depart from the traditional. Furnishings, in addition to those provided by the public purse, have added greatly to the attractiveness of the interior. A very beautiful communion table and canopy has been gifted by the Church of Scotland and matching furniture, including a lectern, choir seats and pew frontals, have been provided by the central fund of PMUB Churches. A baptismal font has been paid for by gifts from the Officers' and Sergeants' Messes and proceeds from a Sale of Work have made it possible to install leaded light windows instead of plain.

The interior wall is brick faced, and there was some initial reaction to this, particularly because the bricks are off white, but the walls are already beginning to look most effective as the bricks mellow to a more natural shade. The floor was originally to be marble grey tiles broken by occasional red tiles, now all grey, as it was felt the red in the floor would protrude too much and clash with the patterned red curtain on which the cross is fixed behind the communion table.

The service on 6 September was conducted by the Rev IE Newell, representing the Baptist and Congregational Churches; the Rev F Douglas Morley, a former Methodist Principal Chaplain, and the dedication was by the very Rev JA Fraser, who represented the Scottish and Presbyterian Churches. Present were Senior Officers of the Royal Air Force, Civic Dignitaries, representatives of the Free Church Council, a number of Service chaplains including the Rev CY McClashan, the Principal Chaplain of the PMUB, together with representatives of the serving airmen, apprentices and their families.

After many difficulties Padre McClashan had managed to obtain an electronic organ and so the opening service and dedication was preceded by an organ recital given by Sgt Patterson, the Church Organist. After that the bell was tolled, and the silence that followed was broken by the Very Rev Fraser's resounding knock and his request 'Let the Door be Opened'. The singing was magnificent, the choir starting with 'Non Nobis Domine', and the short sermon reminded everyone of the meaning of the true church.

There are still things to be done. It is hoped in time to replace the Service issued tubular steel chairs with pews, and there is need to work towards the provision of a Church Hall to replace the old Club Room, which is soon to be demolished.

The interior and exterior of the new church with Padre Schofield

The Dedication

Modern Training

No. 1 in the West (1974)

Although it has no runways and lacks the noise of a military airfield, RAF Locking near Weston-super-Mare (Somerset) is one of the most important training stations in the Royal Air Force. It is here at No. 1 Radio School that the men responsible for servicing the RAF's ground communications and radar installations are trained. The modern RAF is heavily dependent on ground communications and radar and a large number of skilled tradesmen are required to keep this equipment functioning in all conditions. Training at Locking is aimed at producing skilled men capable of understanding, operating and servicing all forms of modern electronic systems.

The standard of training compares favourably with that of modern technical establishments elsewhere in the country and graduate students feel that the mix of theoretical study combined with practical training fits them well for the task they are required to do in the RAF.

The raising of the school leaving age has been one of the factors governing the switch from apprentices to adult students. Adult training has the advantage of attracting more mature students, some of whom may have previously been employed in the electronic industry. This is particularly true of the new Direct Entrant Adult Fitter who is required to have two 'O' levels, in mathematics and a science subject, as a pre-requisite for selection for training.

The training at Locking varies to meet the general and specialist requirements of the ground electronic engineering trade sub-group. The Direct Entrant Mechanic course lasts 16 weeks and on completion the airmen pass out in the rank of Leading or Senior Aircraftman on a five year engagement. They are then employed on servicing equipment appropriate to their specialisation, i.e. communications or radar, but work initially under the supervision of the higher skilled technicians and fitters. The further training course lasts about one year and is designed to train the mechanics with field experience to electronics fitter standard. The Direct Entrant Fitter trains for a little over a year to reach the same standard as that achieved by the craft apprentices on their two year courses. The post-graduate courses of different durations are designed to train qualified tradesmen on equipment not covered previously or specialised equipment of new design. The courses for overseas personnel correspond briefly with the RAF basic mechanic and fitter courses and are directed towards ground radar and communications principles, equipment and technical practices.

The training organisation at Locking is divided into a Student Squadron which looks after the domestic life, discipline, welfare, physical education and general Service training of the students; a Basic Studies Squadron, which as the name implies, is responsible for the teaching of basic theory and general education subjects; and 3 Trade Training Squadrons (Trade Practices, Communications and Radar) which cover

The AR3D Radar

Modern Training

trade technology and workshop training. Each squadron has Service and civilian specialist instructional and supervisory staff.

The teaching of theory in Basic Studies starts from scratch and is supported by locally developed practical training aids. Visual aids are used extensively. There is plenty of practical laboratory work at each stage of the course so that the students theoretical knowledge is properly aligned with his practical application. Students test equipment, record results and have to draw their own conclusions at the end of each laboratory exercise.

The Trade Practices Squadron provides the practical instruction to diagnose and repair faults, using the most up-to-date test equipment. The skills of soldering, assembly of components and correct use of tools is taught. The 'skill of hand' training includes basic fitting - marking, drilling, soldering circuits with mixed components and printed circuit soldering and repair.

Skill of Hand in 4(T) in the 1980s

A project phase is aimed to improve and exercise skills and students may, for example, build themselves hi-fi amplifiers - to be bought at material cost price.

In the Communication and Radar Squadrons a similar training pattern emerges - applied principles followed by practical experiments to acquaint the student with circuitry found in operational equipment. Class work and laboratory work again run in parallel and

Demonstrating the use of a Spectrum Analyser

Over and Out 111

Modern Training

students are set tasks to check the performance of different circuits.

The final stage of fitter training is the Equipment Phase. This lasts 12 to 13 weeks and teaches students to fault-find on equipments similar to that used in service. The correct operation, maintenance, testing and servicing of vital ground equipment is the end result of Locking's training programme.

With the introduction of new applications of computers in the Service, training in digital techniques and computer fundamentals is becoming increasingly important. Training is provided, as appropriate, in basic digital techniques, in computer fundamentals and in programming.

With an ever increasing dependence on 'black box' technology, the task of producing sufficient highly-trained tradesmen to handle this equipment is more important than ever.

Trade Group 3 L Tech Basic Training Patterns (1978)

On Thursday, 12 October 1978, No 1 Radio School RAF Locking passed a significant milestone when the combined class of FTC6 and FAD12, comprising 24 aspiring Telecommunications and Air Defence Electronic Technicians, commenced training in accordance with the newly-designed Trade Group 3 courses. The introduction of these new courses follows closely on the introduction of the new Trade Group 3 on 1 January 1978 which replaces the previous Trade Group 2 Ground Sub-Group. Why was it necessary to re-organise this long established Trade Group 2 Ground and its associated training? Putting it in simple terms, the introduction of complex electronic and data handling equipment into the Royal Air Force during the last 10 years

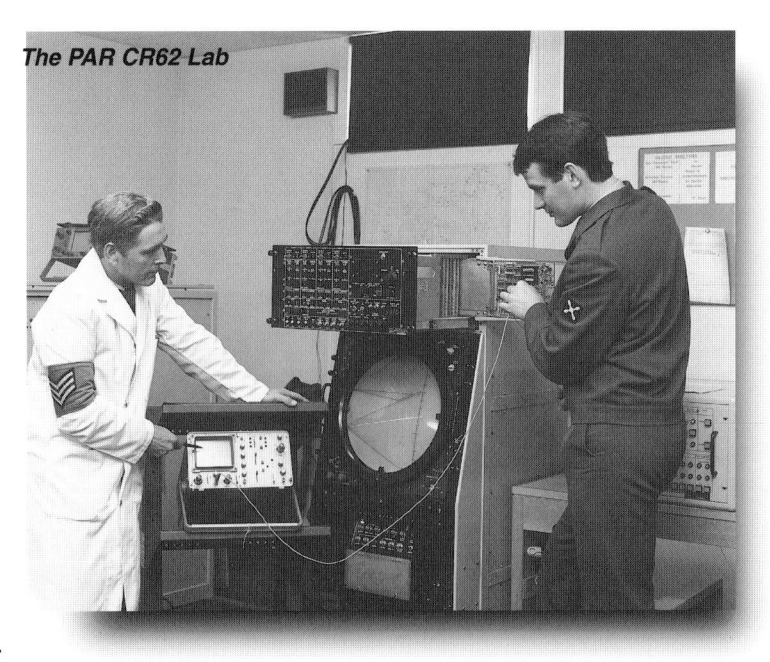

The PAR CR62 Lab

The Passing Out of Direct Entry 5 (Ground Radio) in 1973 (J/T Taylor - third from right in the front row is now OC Training Wing)

112 *Over and Out*

Modern Training

has created a need for more specialist trade boundaries for effective employment patterns. Consequently, training to support these specialist employment areas has had to be reviewed to ensure that it adequately prepares students for their future employment. What are these specialist employment areas and which trades work within them? There are three specialist areas, or operational environments as follows:

a. Air Defence. The L Tech Air Defence (L Tech AD) trade is responsible for maintaining major ground radar systems in the Air Defence Ground Environment (ADGE) including surface-to-air missile (SAM) systems such as Bloodhound and Rapier with their associated data links and ground/air communications.

b. Airfields. The L Tech Airfield (L Tech AF) trade is responsible for maintaining both airfield radar and communications equipments.

c. Telecommunications. The L Tech Telecommunications (L Tech TC) trade is responsible for maintaining high power high frequency (HF) transmitters, HF receivers, satellite communications equipment and associated speech and line telegraphy networks.

From this short summary, it is obvious that Trade group 3 is concerned with a complex electronic engineering task, full of interest and challenge to tradesmen employed within the trade group. It follows that training must be the best available to fit tradesmen to meet this challenge and the new TG3 courses have been designed to meet this objective. How is this training organised and how long are the courses? The diagram shows the various phases of training - let's see what goes on in each phase.

a. Common Phase one. All classes, Direct Entry of Further Training, Airfield, Air Defence or Telecommunications specialisations, commence training in Phase one. This training comprises all the essential elements of mathematics, basic electricity and electronics, servicing and workshop practices which are common to all three trade specialisations The commonality of Phase one training allows the combination in one class of students in two differing trade specialisations. On completion of Phase one training, the class splits into its own trade specialist groups and moves onto the second phase of training.

b. Phase Two Training. Phase two training is specific to the requirements of L Tech AF, AD or TC and commences with instruction on specialist techniques associated with the type of equipment with which AF, AD or TC tradesman will be concerned. This is followed by instruction on a representative set of equipment of the type which tradesmen in each of the trade sub-divisions will encounter when they leave No 1 Radio School to commence employment in the field.

The instructional specifications (IS) now coming into use for TG3 training have been written in accordance with the Systems Approach to Training (SAT). They have been produced by the Course Design Team in close consultation with the management and instructors of each training squadron and their content reflects, therefore, a wide cross-section of expertise and experience in the requirements of equipment maintenance and associated training. Once in use they are further validated and amended through constructive comment by training squadrons at RAF Locking and from external formations such as MOD Trade Standards Section and HQRAFSC.

An associated training task imposed by the introduction of TG3 is that of assimilation training for the previous L Tech AF sub-trade. It is necessary to provide training for L Techs AF(Communications) in radar specialist techniques and airfield radar equipments. Similarly, training must be provided for L Techs AF(Radar) in communications specialist techniques and airfield ground/air communications equipments. This training must be provided for students at present under training as L Techs AF(R) or (C), also for tradesmen currently employed in these interim trades.

For students undergoing training in the interim trades, assimilation training course lengths will be:

L Tech AF(C) to L Tech AF - 15 weeks
L Tech AF(R) to L Tech AF - 13 weeks

For tradesmen currently employed in the L Tech AF interim trades, assimilation training course lengths will be:

L Tech AF(C) to L Tech AF - 17 weeks
L Tech AF(R) to L Tech AF - 18 weeks.

Trade Group 3 L Tech Basic Training Patterns

L Tech AF

Total Course Duration
DE - 66 weeks
FT - 62 weeks

Phase 2 - L Tech AF
(DE = 40 weeks)
(FT = 36 weeks)

Radar and Communications Specialist Techniques

Airfield Radar & Communications Equipments

Workshop Practices

L Tech AD

Total Course Duration
DE - 57 weeks
FT - 53 weeks

Phase 2 - L Tech AD
(DE = 31 weeks)
(FT = 27 weeks)

Radar Specialist Techniques

Airfield Defence Radar Equipments

Workshop Practices

L Tech TC

Total Course Duration
DE - 55 weeks
FT- 51 weeks

Phase 2 - L Tech TC
(DE = 29 weeks)
(FT = 25 weeks)

Telecommunications Specialist Techniques

Telecommunications Equipments

Workshop Practices

Common Phase 1
L Techs AF, AD & TC
(26 weeks)

Recruit Training
(Direct Entry)

SAC L Mech
(Further Training)

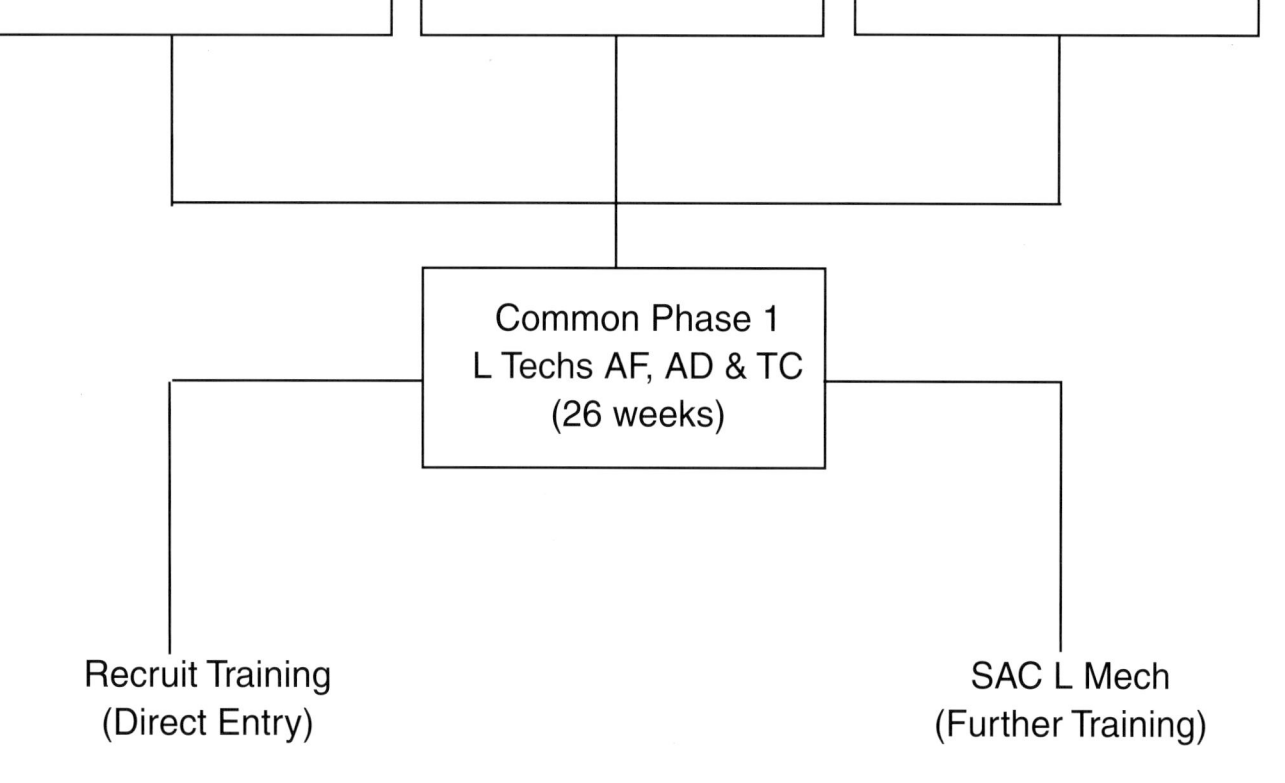

114 *Over and Out*

Thoughts from a Direct Entry Fitter

(Greg Burns)

'It's March 1978. The commencement of six weeks 'square bashing' at RAF Swinderby (then the school of basic recruit training) was made marginally more bearable by the prospect of spending 18 months Direct Entry Fitter training at RAF Locking. For the likes of most of my Entry, from darkest Lancashire and Yorkshire, the name Weston-super-Mare conjured up visions of exotic scantily clad females parading their wares along miles of golden sandy beech. Just imagine our surprise when we discovered that Weston was the wheelchair capital of Western Europe! And as for the beach, well you've been there.

Walking through the gates of the Station for the first time was like entering a meeting of the United Nations. In addition to the RAF personnel there were members of the Armed Forces of Kenya, Nigeria, Malaya, Oman, Jordan and even Scotland. This is in deference to one of our group who was a staunch Scottish Nationalist. He insisted that his fair flower of a country had been raped, pillaged and plundered by the low life Saxons for the best part of five centuries. This is somewhat strange when one considers that he was of Polish descent! As far as I know he is still serving and still expressing his outrage to anyone who will listen.

The accommodation for the general trainee population of the time was 18 man rooms. Some courses were lucky enough to be in the more modern four man roomed accommodation blocks. What luxury!

Wherever you were though the floor, and everything else for that matter, was always polished to such a degree (by us I might add) that you could have used it for shaving. I remember that the central heating system was thoroughly unreliable and we spent long periods during the winter of 1979 with no heating whatsoever. The presence of a half inch thick layer of ice on the windows was a regular occurrence. This was on the inside!

Our days were filled with the business of learning. For the vast majority of trainees this was fairly mundane stuff (just like being back at school) and it was relatively uncommon for anyone to fail exams. 3(T) and 4(T) blocks were the centres of excellence for basic electronics and workshop practice subjects. This was where we learned how to electrocute ourselves and take the tops off our fingers. It has to be said though we did it with style. 2(T) was responsible for radar and airfield equipment and 1(T) looked after the telecommunications and larger radio equipment training. There were also, of course, regular sessions of PT. It always appeared to us that the sadistic gits in the posh white vests and skin tight tracksuit bottoms felt that it was their God given life mission to select ridicule and publicly humiliate the less physically coordinated members of the trainee population. Coincidentally, they were remarkably adept in this their preferred pastime. Good character building stuff.

The modern bed space

The food was served up in the recently opened Quantock Mess and was generally of pretty good standard especially when considering that it had to feed over 2,000 people at each sitting. We always wondered whether or not there was any truth to the rumour that the Mess put bromide in the tea and coffee. Eventually, we decided that it was probably the lack of available (and acceptable) local talent that curbed our desires in this direction so we just accepted it as a fact of life.

Staying with the Mess for a moment, I remember the occasion when one of the Jordanian trainees had done something to upset a member of one of the other courses. The response was for the offended party to paint the Star of David on the front of the Airmens' Mess. This resulted in the whole Jordanian contingent refusing to go anywhere near the Mess let alone eat in it. Fortunately, it happened during the festival of Ramadam so the appearance of the symbol removed any temptation there might have been to break the fast.

When we first arrived at Locking there seemed relatively little to occupy ourselves with during the evening. However, this was to change. The NAAFI (Roundel Club) disco began to get quite a following, not only among the trainees but also the local ladies, so much so that people would make a point of returning from a weekend away early enough to get well and truly shedded on a Sunday evening. It was also the place to be if you wanted a fight. I apologise beforehand for the following but I'm just relating the story. As I've already mentioned Locking housed a mixed race society including Nigerians. Well, one bold lad thought that it would be a good idea to ask one of the Nigerians if his name was Rastus just to see what the reaction would be. He obviously wasn't aware that the Nigerian people are sworn enemies of the Rastafarians and that the chap concerned would take this as the ultimate insult. All hell broke loose! Blood, teeth, beer and furniture all over the place. The only lad in the room who did not suffer some form of injury was the one who asked the question in the first place! He was cowering in the corner of the room trying manfully to protect his pint from being spilled!

Dangerous

That story apart, there was never any form of racial tension at Locking and, generally, all of the trainees, whatever their background, got on extremely well. This is more than can be said for the relationship between the trainees and the local youth. At one stage it became quite dangerous for a trainee to walk the streets of Weston on his own and a number of lads were quite severely beaten. One to the extent that he was medically discharged from the Service because of a fractured skull.

Personal transport was, for the most part, conspicuous by its absence. Very few people owned cars and those that did could make a few quid on the side running an impromptu taxi service into the town. One lad had a Ford Cortina MK II with dodgy engine mountings. If he pulled away too quickly from stationary then the engine would jump its mountings and rotate along the axis of the drive shaft. It was a regular occurrence to see the occupants of the car leaping out at traffic lights to re-seat the engine in order to continue the journey.

Returning to the Roundel Club. This was where the vast majority of the public telephones were housed and there was always an enormous queue to use them. Homesick, lovesick or just plain sick individuals would wait for hours to make a phone call. Quite often, after waiting all this time, they would find that the payphone was full and couldn't be used! Most amusing unless you were the one affected. There was a 'sticky bun' in the Club which sold all sorts of goodies at extortionate NAAFI prices. However, as it was the only place to go we were a captive audience. They

'There were also, of course, regular sessions of PT. It always appeared to us that the sadistic gits in the posh white vests and skin tight tracksuit bottoms felt that it was their God given life mission to select, ridicule and humiliate the less physically coordinated members of the trainee population.'

A modern view of the Station looking towards 1(T) Block. Note the Sandes Home in the foreground now demolished

also had a number of gaming machines in the place which were usually occupied by the Bell Fruit Brigade. Some people put so much money into the things that they are probably still paying off the debts today!

Generally speaking crime was not a major problem. It was taken for granted that petty theft was an occupational hazard. Leaving your rain coat in the Airmen's Mess or your belongings in the drying rooms was an open invitation to the opportunist thief who in all probability had had something of his own reappropriated beforehand. There must be someone out there with hundreds of RAF rain coats! Perhaps the most serious offence which occurred during my time was the theft and fraudulent use of a lad's cheque book. The lad concerned was on the sister course to mine and it transpired that the culprit was someone from my course. Needless to say he received absolutely no sympathy when he was caught and it was a relief to all of us when he was dismissed from the Service.

We sat our final practical examination on the morning after our end of course party which proved to be a disastrous mistake on the part of the programme planners. High voltage equipment and drunken airmen definitely do not mix. Several of us were rather the worse for wear and periodically interrupted the examiner's assessment by rushing off to the toilets to be sick. We returned ashen faced and shaking. It was difficult enough trying to concentrate on remaining upright let alone on the complexities of a high voltage transmitter. Fortunately we all managed to get through the ordeal.

With completion of our course came the Passing Out Ceremony at which we were presented with our certificates and got the opportunity to show off our newly acquired J/T badges. Looking back this was one of the proudest moments of my life and I know that the feeling is shared by many of my colleagues. I have returned to Locking on numerous occasions since and these visits have never failed to bring back a 'face from the past', all of whom have a special regard for the place. As one of my friends once eloquently put it 'as I slide down the bannister of life, RAF Locking is a splinter in my backside that I never quite seem able to remove'. And so say all of us!'

A Day in the Life of an Airman (AD 1990)

(Tongue firmly in cheek)

After marching for fully two minutes we arrived at the refuse disposal point. The course halted in the usual ragged manner which didn't surprise me in the least. After disposing of the rubbish I noted that several of my course had cans which contained an alcoholic beverage. I reminded them that under Station Standing Orders, Part two, Para 54, Section B - alcohol must not be consumed in a barrack block.

We arrived at our place of duty at 0805 hrs and attempted to sit quietly while awaiting our instructor. But as usual certain members of the course let us down. At 0820hrs precisely I took it upon myself to look for our instructor as no one else seemed the slightest bit interested. I proceeded to his office and discovered to my amazement that he was still sitting down at his desk engrossed in the same books that I had been studying the night before. It occurred to me that he was hastily studying the part of the syllabus that we were about to cover. I announced my presence to the officer and informed him that he was 13 minutes late for the start of our lesson. He hastily gathered his books and followed me to the classroom where I brought the class smartly to attention and waited for him to tell us to sit easy.

Monotonous

The lesson finally commenced and the dull and monotonous tones of the instructor soon sent some of the unwilling students to sleep, which surprised me because transistor theory seemed most interesting to me! I awoke the airman sitting next to me only to be promptly reprimanded by the instructor for not paying attention.

Late

Time soon passed and before I knew it, it was 1000 hrs and I pointed out to the instructor that we were five minutes late for our entitled morning break, as laid down in Station Standing Orders, Part two, Para 13 - daily routine for permanent staff, instructors and students. Realising his mistake and following his own principles on man management he dismissed us for our break.

I tidied myself, placed my beret on my head, and marched on the left hand side of the road to the disciplinary office to collect the morning mail, and signed the appropriate book. I proceeded to leave the room when I was stopped by the Discip Sergeant who told me that I needed a neck shave. This surprised me since I had only had a neck shave several days ago.

On getting back to the classroom I noticed that I was three minutes late, I apologised but no comment was made as the instructor realised his mistake earlier in the morning. The lesson started and at 1100 hrs several of the class started to make comments that they were thirsty. I pointed out that under Station Standing Orders there is no break entitlement at 1100 hrs. The instructor thanked me for my intervention and continued with the lesson until 1155 hrs when we were dismissed from the class to proceed to the Mess for dinner.

The Basic Course Directory since 1966

Dates	Title	Length	Students	Remarks
May 66 - Dec 82	Ground Radar - Non MOD	50 wks	116	Foreign students
Mar 67 - Aug 86	Electronic Fitter Ground Radar - Overseas Airmen	53 wks	715	Foreign students
Feb 68 - May 86	Electronic Fitter Ground Communications - Overseas Airmen	53 wks	450	Foreign students
Oct 67 - May 86	Electronic Fitter Ground Communications	45 wks	1060	Further training SAC to J/T - LFittGC
March 68 - July 78	Electronic Fitter Ground Radar	50-60 wks	720	Further training SAC to J/T - LFittGR
Sep 68 - July 78	El Mech Ground Communications	16 wks	900	SAC mechanic LMechGC
Nov 68 - July 77	El Mech Radar	16 wks	900	SAC Mechanic LMechGR
Dec 69 - Mar 81	El Mech Ground Radar Overseas Airmen	16 wks	280	Foreign students
Jan 72 - Oct 79	Direct Entry Fitter Ground Radar	53 wks	500	DE fitter LFittGR
July 72 - July 79	Direct Entry Fitter Ground Communications	53 wks	369	DE fitter LFittGC
July 76 - Feb 85	Direct Entry Fitter Synthetic Trainer	53 wks	620	DE fitter LFittST
Dec 76 - July 93	Direct Entry El Tech - Airfield	53 wks	874	Single skill DE fitter LTechAF
Dec 76 - April 93	Direct Entry El Tech - Air Defence	53 wks	1073	Single skill DE fitter LTechAD
Feb 77 - Nov 94	Direct Entry El Tech - Telecommunications	53 wks	1429	Single skill DE fitter LTechTC
Jan 78 - Nov 81	El Mech - Ground Communications for Overseas Airmen	16 wks	165	Foreign students
Mar 78 - July 92	El Mech - Telecommunications	16 wks	515	Single skill mechanic LMechTC
Mar 78 - Jan 93	El Mech - Air Defence	24 wks	298	Single skill mechanicLMechAD
Mar 78 - Apr 93	El Mech - Airfields	16 wks	512	Single skill mechanic LMech AF
Jun 78 - Mar 94	Further training El Tech Air Defence	53 wks	445	SAC to J/T LTech AD
Jul 78 - Mar 94	Further training El Tech Airfield	53 wks	437	SAC to J/T Tech AF
Jul 78 - Jun 94	Further training El Tech Telecommunications	53 wks	517	SAC to J/T LTechTC
Jun 93 - present	Basic Training El Mech	30 wks	96	Multi skill mechanic
Nov 94 - present	Further Training Eng Tech El	40 wks	72	SAC to J/T Eng Tech EL
Mar 89 - present	Telecommunications Operator (Basic)	23 wks	815	Trade Group 11 SAC TCO
Jul 89 - Jan 92	Telecommunications Operator(conversion)	16 wks	152	Trade Group 11 SAC TCO conversion to morse

Operation Burberry 1977/78

Operation Burberry was the code name given to the Armed Forces work in allaying the worst effects of the Fireman's Strike in 1977/78. RAF Locking was involved from 14 November 1977 to 15 June 1978. The ORB records that what was initially seen as a fairly low key involvement rapidly expanded to a major operation. RAF Locking was responsible for the reception, kitting and despatch of many hundreds of airmen operating a stand in fire service in the old Avon area. Furthermore, until a local authority alternative was established, RAF Locking provided command and control for operations. To judge the scale of this effort Supply Squadron alone recorded over 1,000 hours overtime in the two months mid November to mid January.

The Weston Flood Disaster

13 December 1981

On Sunday evening Weston-super-Mare and District suffered a disastrous flood as a result of a high tide and Force 10 winds which caused enormous damage to property and sea defences and rendered many people homeless.

Soon after the disaster struck RAF Locking was called upon to assist as Aid to Civil Powers and sprang into action to bring relief to stricken families.

Sea defences were breached as the wind suddenly changed from south east to Force 10 westerly late on 13 December. Just after midnight, using the station's MT, personnel assisted in the evacuation of householders at Uphill, Sand Bay, Kingston Seymour and Wick St Lawrence. They also used two inflatable powered dinghies - the Station Sailing Club's rescue boats.

The Sea Front at Weston

After the first high tide had ebbed, RAF personnel spent three hours filling sand bags on the beach at Weston.

It was a race against time in the face of the next high tide with the men working frantically at 5am with the next high water due at 8am. Fortunately the tide did not bring such serious flooding and there was an appreciable drop in the force of the wind. Nevertheless, the RAF filled 7,500 sandbags in this early morning operation.

More than 100 personnel were involved in repairing sea defences at Uphill and clearing roads for emergency services to get through. In many areas entire garden walls had been lifted and deposited across roads by the flood water and cars were left in heaps, several on top of each other.

As 2,000 tons of rock were being shuttled into the area by lorries to repair the sea wall, the RAF again set to work to build a sandbag wall between houses and the again threatening sea. They also removed carpets from 100 houses and took them back to RAF Locking for cleaning and drying. The Arctic

The Weston Flood Disaster

Some of Locking's Sandbags

weather created problems with the saturated carpets freezing to the concrete. Manoeuvring the carpets was not an easy task as they were so heavy with sea water and mud it took up to 10 men just to lift one carpet.

Following the emergency, as flood water receded, RAF personnel helped with the clearing up and later, on a voluntary basis, an aid programme was established to redecorate old people's homes in Uphill.

As the Local Authority exhausted all possible temporary accommodation for evacuees some 20 families were welcomed as house guests by RAF families in married quarters.

After the event there were many letters and calls expressing thanks for the efforts of RAF personnel, a feeling which is summed up in the letter of appreciation from the Mayor and the Loose Minute from Under Secretary of State (Air Force) to the Chief of the Air Staff.

Uphill in Flood

Cars piled high in Uphill

Drying Carpets

Letter of appreciation from the Mayor

Mayor's Parlour,
Grove House, Grove Park.
Weston-super-Mare.
BS23 2QJ
Telephone 32567
23 December 1981

Group Captain D.G.Harrington, C.Eng. RAF.
Officer Commanding,
Royal Air Force,
Locking,
Weston-super-Mare.

Dear Dave

Flood Disaster. Weston-super-Mare. 13/12/81

The horrific flooding and terrible weather conditions that hit the west this last weekend, as we are all aware, has caused enormous distress, and I now write on behalf of the townspeople of Weston-super-Mare to express their gratitude, as well as my own, for the enormous assistance rendered by all those Officers and men under your command to those people who were so deeply affected.

Within a very short period of time your Royal Air Force Contingent under the command of Wing Commander Geoffrey Findley, had brought into Weston, and particularly the stricken Uphill sector, considerable supplies and equipment, and worked alongside the other services under appalling conditions. The availability and use of your married quarters was also a valuable contribution.

Weston-super-Mare will be forever grateful to all on your Station who so quickly gave the Town the aid it so needed at such a critical time, thereby adding a further chapter to the very special relationship which has existed for so long between R.A.F. Locking, Weston-super-Mare.

Please convey the heartfelt thanks of the citizens of Weston-super-Mare, coupled with my own, to all at R.A.F. Locking, who helped Weston so nobly in its time of need.

Kindest regards
Jim
Town Mayor.

PARLIAMENTARY UNDER-SECRETARY OF STATE
FOR THE ARMED FORCES

LOOSE MINUTE

D/US of S(AF)/JW/3/1/1/1

CAS

ROYAL AIR FORCE LOCKING

I felt I must record my thanks for all the work the officers and men of Royal Air Force Locking have done in Weston-Super-Mare under very difficult conditions over the last few days. They have been of considerable help to my constituents and their sterling work can only have enhanced the Royal Air Force's already high reputation in the area.

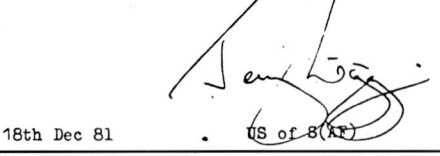

18th Dec 81   US of S(AF)

Flowerdown Fair

A midsummer annual Flowerdown Fair was started in 1971 to provide an open day for the public at which the RAF could show off its mettle and also raise money for charitable organisations, notably the Royal Air Force Benevolent Fund and Royal Air Force Association. Previous to this RAF Locking had, on occasions, been selected to provide an open day in September under the guise of the 'Battle of Britain At Home Days'.

Battle of Britain Memorial Flight Poster

122 *Over and Out*

Initially Flowerdown Fair was a homespun event but as the years passed it became ever more ambitious eventually providing a full arena and flying programmes together with a full supporting cast of a fairground, sideshows, some of which remained homespun, and fast food outlets. Entrance cost was always kept low to encourage families and children were entertained by a tour of the Station in a 'Noddy Train' operated by MT which started its work in 1974.

Dads were looked after with a beer tent run by volunteers which always proved a successful money spinner.

Flowerdown Fair continued until 1996 when reductions in personnel forced its demise. Some facts extracted from the ORB show its growth:

July 1974 - £2,000 raised for charity. Flypast by the last operational Lancaster.

June 1982 - £7,500 raised for charity by 6,000 visitors.

Locking Air Display

Locking's Flowerdown Fair raises money for local and Royal Air
rities. This year in excess of £11,000 was raised. The highlight of
ernoon was the Air Display and the undoubted 'stars' were the
historic Battle of Britain Flight.
commemorate the 48th anniversary of the Battle of Britain, we
ire a poster of the historic trio — Spitfire, Hurricane and Lancaster.

Flowerdown Fair

I Wanna be a Fighter Pilot — *'So do I', says Police Dog Rex*

July 1984 - £10,000 raised for charity by 15,000 visitors.

A report on the Flowerdown Fair 1974 records that 'some 8,000 people assembled on the cricket field and its surrounds to enjoy a spectacular flying display, listen to the band, sample the fun of the fair and spend their pay rises on good charitable causes. The national stand-by at Service establishments did not put a cursory end to the flying display or cause abandonment of the whole open day, as happened to both Royal Navy and Army events on the same day. And fortunately the weather cleared in good time to afford watchers an excellent view of the Swords and Red Arrows. Weston-super-Mare Concert Band gave two performances during the afternoon and there was a Karate Demonstration, a display by the Mounted Division of the Somerset and Avon Police and a parade of the Banwell Harriers in the arena.

The stall holders and fund raisers were extremely busy, few having much time to draw breath. Several suffered notably in the cause; Padre Tasker (CE) being submerged so often in the ducking pool that some wondered whether he might contemplate conversion! One husband spent most money trying to 'ditch' his wife but doubtless the lady concerned will extract her particular form of revenge in due course.

Over 1,600 cars were parked within the camp boundary, apart from the fee dodgers who parked on the verges of the main road, and altogether the gross taking exceeded £3,000.'

The RAF Locking Continuity Drill Team

Flowerdown Fair

Flowerdown Fair 1996 - From the Air

Ode to Flowerdown

Locking Ladies by the score,
Soft drinks and warm canned beer,
Children scream and aircraft roar
For Flowerdown Fair is here !

Circus tents erected,
Sweeties by the ton,
Lost children look dejected
Under the noon-day sun.

Parachutes descended
in another spot -
the flight plan was amended
(or the pilot just forgot).

Choppers giving joy rides
Others on display,
Excitement raged on all sides.
Oh what a super day.

Cakes and buns and cookies:
Teddies by the score:
Magazines and goodies.
You couldn't ask tor more.

So after months of preparation
Only memories now remain,
And quiet contemplation
Till it's Flowerdown time again!

Anon.

Aerobatics viewed from the Arena

The RAFA Stall in 1996 with the present Station Commander Gp Capt Rooms

Over and Out 125

FLOWERDO

**Flowerdown Fair is RAF Locking's ma
RAF and local charities. This month we
we hope to feature pi**

◀ Bowling for half a pig.

▼ All aboard the Flowerdown Expre

◀ Balancing act.

◀ King of the bouncy castle!

126 *Over and Out*

WN FAIR '88

...ent of the year, all proceeds going to
...ure 'all the fun of the fair'. Next month
...s of the Air Display.

Happy landings. ▶

◀ *Take that!*

▼ *Pedal power.*

...ee! Look
...ne!

◀ *In perfect formation.*

Over and Out 127

The BSAD Wheelchair Marathon

> **ROYAL AIR FORCE LOCKING**
> **& THE SOUTH WEST REGION OF**
> **THE BRITISH SPORTS ASSOCIATION FOR THE DISABLED**
> will hold a
> **Sponsored Wheelchair Fun Marathon**
> with units of the Royal Navy, Army and the Royal Air Force in the South West
>
> ON SUNDAY 2nd OCTOBER 1983
> AT ROYAL AIR FORCE LOCKING,
> Nr WESTON-SUPER-MARE
>
> TEAMS CONSISTING OF THREE SERVICEMEN PUSHING A DISABLED PERSON IN A WHEELCHAIR PROPOSE TO RACE OVER THE MARATHON DISTANCE OF 26 MILES 385 YARDS AT THIS EVENT.
>
> PLEASE SPONSOR THE EFFORTS OF "PUSHERS" AND "PUSHED" TO RAISE MONEY FOR THE SOUTH WEST REGION OF THE B.S.A.D.
>
> **Advertisement for Participants in 1983**

In 1982 an event called the BSAD Wheelchair Marathon was started in aid of the British Sports Association for the Disabled and continued until 1996 when force reductions within the Armed Forces generally caused its demise. The BSAD is a relatively small body who provide a variety of sporting opportunities for the enjoyment, and rehabilitation, of its members.

Teams of three runners push a disabled person in a wheelchair around a 26 mile 365 yard marathon distance - 10 laps of a 2.6 mile course, the runners operating as a relay team and the disabled person being the baton. Entry for teams was open to any service or cadet unit in the loosely defined south west of England.

The objectives of the event were to give disabled people an enjoyable and exciting day out; to forge links between disabled groups and the military and thirdly to raise money for the

Army Air Corps Handing Over in 1988

128   Over and Out

charity through sponsorship of the teams.

Large numbers of very diverse teams enter, for example, in 1987 there were 94 teams and it was won by members of the Army Physical Training Corps then serving with No 1 Para in a time of two hours 38 minutes. In 1991 there were 61 teams and the event was won by RAF Hereford in two hours 36 minutes, second was a Royal Marine team and third RAF Locking's first team.

Some Teams compete in fancy dress

The first Locking team home in 1991

Coming down the hill to the finish

Noteworthy events of the time

In June 1983 plans were revealed to use the redundant Bellman Hangars for the storage of a pre-fabricated United States Naval Hospital which would be erected and operated from RAF Locking in a future conflict.

On 11 February 1985 a coach crash in Germany involving the RAFG Band resulted in many casualties, with 19 fatalities. This loss was keenly felt at RAF Locking as several of those killed and injured had recently served in the Western Band. In April 1985 at a service of commemoration five maple trees, donated by the Coach House Inn in Locking Village, were planted next to the Bandroom, together with a plaque to commemorate the loss.

In January 1987 RAF Locking assisted the Local Authority in coping with the worst effects of the 'big freeze'.

In May 1988 RAF Locking was presented with the Royal Air Force Benevolent Fund Jubilee Sword for its efforts in fund raising over the previous year when the Station raised £12,000.

In 1989 RAF Locking raised £32,000 for all its charities.

In May 1990 trainees, as part of a community project, rebuilt the landing steps on Steep Holm which had been destroyed by the winter gales. The airlift of materials was carried out by a Chinook from 33 Squadron. Had this work not been done, visitors would not have been able to land and income to the Kenneth Allsop Trust critically reduced.

Noteworthy events

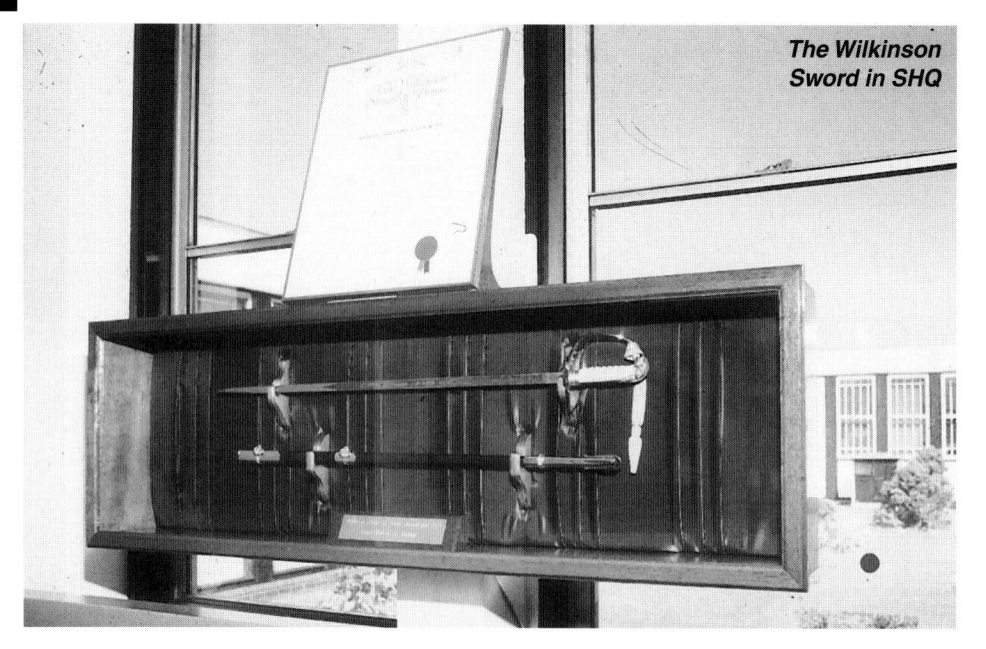

On 7 December 1990 RAF Locking was awarded the Wilkinson Sword for Peace which is awarded annually 'to the station which in the previous year has done most for the community in which it is based'. The occasion was marked by a parade of 900 airmen/women and a fly-past.

The Gulf Families Support Group was set up at RAF Locking on 15 January 1991 to provide support to the families of all three Services living in the local area whose relations were serving in the Gulf War.

The aims of the Support Group were to maintain contact and provide a channel for communications, offer a meeting place for families and provide a link to established welfare services. The volunteers received over 150 offers of help ranging from nursing to baby sitting.

There were over 2,000 telephone calls from local people wanting to send mail or parcels to Servicemen and the Station received gifts weighing over nine tons, valued at £22,000, which had to be sorted, packed and addressed for airlift to the Gulf.

In February 1993 the ORB records the visit of a survey team to examine the future strategy for airman's ground training in the RAF with a view to closing one of the three training schools.

On 29 May 1993 RAF Locking was used to stage a Dambusters Spectacular Concert to commemorate the 617 Squadron raid 50 years earlier. It promised to be a truly memorable occasion but unfortunately the May weather intervened and reduced attendance.

Also 1993 saw the 50th Anniversary of No 1 Radio School which had been formed at RAF Cranwell in 1943, moving to RAF Locking in 1950. A 50th Anniversary Booklet was published and a Hangar Dance was held to celebrate the anniversary and support RAFA.

Finally, on 30 October 1997 the Station hosted the BBC Antiques Roadshow.

The Wilkinson Sword in SHQ

Parading the Sword

The Wilkinson Sword Parade

The Reviewing Officer, Air Chief Marshal Sir David Parry-Evans meets SAC(W) Fuller

130   Over and Out

Noteworthy events

The Glenn Miller Night Hangar Dance

The Dambusters Spectacular

Hugh Scully with the World War Two Enigma Machine

The Antiques Roadshow in 3(T)

Over and Out 131

ROYAL AIR FORCE LOCKING

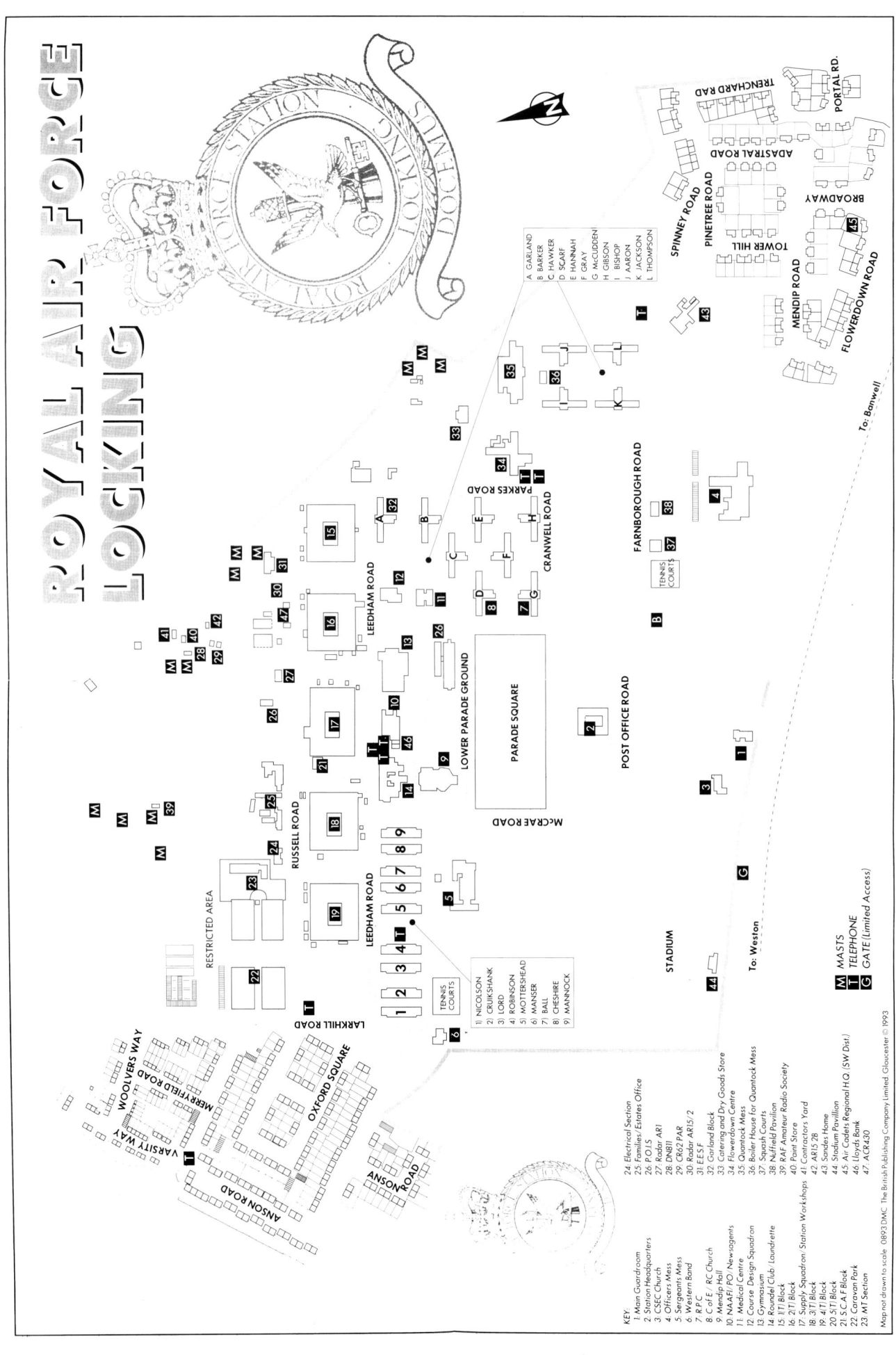

KEY:
1. Main Guardroom
2. Station Headquarters
3. CSEC Church
4. Officers Mess
5. Sergeants Mess
6. Western Band
7. RPC
8. C of E / RC Church
9. Mendip Hall
10. NAAFI/PO Newsagents
11. Medical Centre
12. Course Design Squadron
13. Gymnasium
14. Roundel Club/Laundrette
15. 1(T) Block
16. 2(T) Block
17. Supply Squadron/Station Workshops
18. 3(T) Block
19. 4(T) Block
20. 5(T) Block
21. S.C.A.F Block
22. Caravan Park
23. MT Section
24. Electrical Section
25. Families/Estates Office
26. P.O.I.S
27. Radar AR1
28. DN811
29. CR62 PAR
30. Radar AR15/2
31. E.E.S.F
32. Garland Block
33. Catering and Dry Goods Store
34. Flowerdown Centre
35. Quantock Mess
36. Boiler House for Quantock Mess
37. Squash Courts
38. Nuffield Pavilion
39. RAF Amateur Radio Society
40. Paint Store
41. Contractors Yard
42. AR15 2B
43. Sandes Home
44. Stadium Pavillion
45. Air Cadets Regional H.Q. (SW Dist)
46. Lloyds Bank
47. ACR430

1) NICOLSON
2) CRUIKSHANK
3) LORD
4) ROBINSON
5) MOTTERSHEAD
6) MANSER
7) BALL
8) CHESHIRE
9) MANNOCK

A. GARLAND
B. BARKER
C. HAWKER
D. SCARF
E. HANNAH
F. GRAY
G. McCUDDEN
H. GIBSON
I. BISHOP
J. AARON
K. JACKSON
L. THOMPSON

M MASTS
T TELEPHONE
G GATE (Limited Access)

Map not drawn to scale 0893 DMC The British Publishing Company Limited Gloucester © 1993

Layout drawing - RAF Locking in 1993

132 Over and Out

Our Airmen

(extracted from the Weston Mercury and Somerset Herald - 22 September 1945)

'It was in the early weeks of 1939 that the first trickle of trainees started to arrive at the half-completed RAF School of Technical Training at Locking. We were living in a world of rumours. The fires of war smouldered everywhere. In less than nine months the flames burst forth crackling and roaring across Europe. When the next September came round, nations had tottered, and Britain stood alone against the greatest assembly of military might in history. The world thought we were finished, but we waited calmly and confidently for the blow to fall, and our airmen, the Immortal Few, were shooting in hundreds from English skies the vultures that would have picked the carcase of Empire.

The young men who came to Locking Camp in those early days before the war could have had no idea of what the future held in store. They, and their comrades of other stations, gave no thought to the fact that civilisation's fate would be in their keeping.

Locking Camp, since its opening, has trained many thousands of airmen; its share in the glory of the RAF is considerable. It produced Battle of Britain heroes. Its 'old boys', those light-hearted lads who once walked our streets, mixed with us in our pubs, danced with us, or took our girls to the cinemas, went away to strike terror in our enemies in the far corners of the earth. Many of them have joined the hosts of those for whom 'the Present has latched its postern behind their tremulous stay.'

Privileged

Locking Camp is a self-contained community, a miniature town, on Weston's outskirts, and since the war only a few privileged residents have seen it from the inside. But on Saturday, the 5th anniversary of the RAF's 'best day' in the Battle of Britain, the public were welcomed at the Camp, and despite difficulties of transport, many hundreds of Westonians accepted the invitation.

Prosperity

It was a happy gesture, for there exists many links between Weston and the Camp which only the necessary restrictions of wartime prevented from being more finely cemented. Many of its officers and instructors have made homes in our town; the rank and file have added to our prosperity by supporting our entertainments and trades, and the constantly changing personnel of the Camp has resulted in thousands of men getting to know the district who might never have come here otherwise. We hope to see them, and their wives and families, returning here for holidays in the pleasant days of peace.

Above all, Weston will ever be grateful to the officers and men of Locking, and the Wings stationed in the town itself, who came to the Borough's rescue during the air raids. Sufficient credit has not yet been given to the work that the RAF did during those two grim nights in 1942. Hundreds of airmen helped to extinguish fire bombs, rescue trapped persons, clear debris, and tend to the injured and dying.

Throughout the war, too, there has always been the closest cooperation between the RAF and the civil authorities in defence matters. Thank you, Locking!'

Strong links

The sentiments expressed by the editor in 1945 remain valid to this very day and, in fact, could have been written yesterday using different examples. The people representing RAF Locking over the years have always endeavoured firstly to play their part in the defence of the realm, but secondly to weld strong links to the community so that we, in the Royal Air Force, can contribute positively to the lives of all the people in this local area.

This tribute is a fitting place to conclude this History of Royal Air Force Locking.'

134   Over and Out

Acknowledgements

With special thanks to all those people below who contributed their memories, photographs and other material. It was always intended that this book would tell the history of Royal Air Force Locking through the eyes of the people who served here. Without the efforts of all the contributors this book could never have been written and the story never told.

Peter Adams	JM Moore
Rex Austen	Mr JW Murphy
Les Boot	RWJ Newland
George Burville	Bob Owen
Anthony Butler	Mr Pearn
Dick Cheesman	EH Read
Brian Dobbins	Dougie Reid
Alex Dow	Stan Richardson
John Dunn	CG Roberts
Julian Evans	Mr Rogers
Leonard Fisher	Colin Secker
Mike Fiske	Rev E Philip Schofield
Mike Furness	Roy Schofield
Peter Gill	John Shaw
AME Gillett	Harold Skane
Mrs Goold	Peter Squires
Chris Horn	Paul Tuffrey
Tony Horry	Joe Warn
Vic Huxley	Robin White
Roger Lancaster	Mrs Williams
Bill Larder	Mr GG Williams
Mr Trevor (Nobby) Marwood	Mr TD Williams
Ian Mclaren	Mike Yates
Phil Mills	

Thanks

Thanks are also due to the Daily Mail, Bristol Evening Post and the Weston and Somerset Mercury for allowing material first printed in those newspapers to be used in this book.